INTERNATIONAL SOCIALISM ★

A quarterly journal of socialist theory

Spring 1

GW00725859

Conten

Issue 74 of INTERNATIONAL SOCIALISM, quarterly journal of the Socialist Workers Party (Britain)

Published March 1997
Copyright © International Socialism
Distribution/subscriptions: International Socialism,
PO Box 82, London E3.
American distribution: B de Boer, 113 East Center St, Nutley,
New Jersey 07110.
Subscriptions and back copies: PO Box 16085, Chicago
Illinois 60616
Editorial and production: 0171-538 0538
Sales and subscriptions: 0171-538 5821
American sales: 773 665 7337

ISBN 1 898876 24 X

Printed by BPCC Wheatons Ltd, Exeter, England
Typeset by East End Offset, London E3 3LH

Cover design by Tim Sanders and Steve Bassindale

For details of back copies see the end pages of this book

Subscription rates for one year (four issues) are:

Britain and overseas (surface):	individual	£14.00 ($30)
	institutional	£25.00
Air speeded supplement:	North America	nil
	Europe/South America	£2.00
	elsewhere	£4.00

Note to contributors
The deadline for articles intended for issue 76 of
International Socialism is 1 August 1997

All contributions should be double-spaced with wide margins.
Please submit two copies. If you write your contribution
using a computer, please also supply a disk, together with
details of the computer and programme used.

INTERNATIONAL SOCIALISM ★

A quarterly journal of socialist theory

THE ELECTION campaign in Britain will undoubtedly feature education as one of its crucial battlegrounds—despite the fact that the Tories and Labour are increasingly agreed about the solutions to the crisis in our schools. But are they right? Is the newly dominant right wing critique of 'trendy teaching methods' accurate? Colin Sparks charts the real contours of the crisis in education, looks for its origins in the contradictory needs of the capitalist system and traces how these reflect themselves in the political arena.

INFORMATION TECHNOLOGY is an issue which produces a wide spectrum of responses ranging from the belief that it will usher in a new age of liberty to the fear that it will become the most powerful weapon that our oppressors have yet developed. Colin Wilson untangles the web of misinformation about the internet and examines the limits and possibilities of the technology.

NICARAGUA'S REVOLUTION has been a *cause célebre* on the left for many years, as Ken Loach's recent film *Carla's Song* bears witness. But the left has failed to confront the weakness of the Sandinistas' strategy argues Mike Gonzalez.

CHRISTOPHER HILL examines David Underdown's new account of the English Revolution of the 17th century in the first of our book reviews, while Peter Morgan looks at Nigel Harris's new book on immigration and the global economy, and Alex Callinicos replies to criticisms of his account of materialism and evolution published in *International Socialism* 73.

NOAM CHOMSKY'S work is widely admired among socialists, and rightly so, argues Anthony Arnove in the first of our new occasional series, 'In perspective'. But, he concludes, Chomsky's undoubted achievements shouldn't blind us to the weaknesses of his analysis and his corresponding difficulties in answering the question, 'What is to be done?'

The Tories, Labour and the education crisis

COLIN SPARKS

Introduction

Every day the papers carry some new story about the crisis in education: children are excluded from class; a school is closed for falling standards; Ofsted claims reading levels are too low; the Tories attack teachers and promise more selection; Labour agrees with the Tories; Tony Blair says kids should have homework at seven years old. The Tories say they should have it at six. If you believed the papers and the politicians, everything is wrong in the schools and it is all the fault of teachers, aided by irresponsible single parents. Child centred learning and comprehensive education were mad ideas dreamed up by red teachers back in the 1960s. They have totally failed the nation. Schools churn out uneducated and unemployable young people with no values and no sense of discipline.

The remedy is to return to the traditional methods and the traditional content. Silent, attentive classes, all concentrating on the one teacher who drills the obedient pupils in how to do long division without the aid of a calculator, and a good flogging for those who get the wrong answers, will transform Britain. Unemployment will vanish. Social order will be re-established. The shattered family will be restored. The economy will boom. Britain will sink back into that white, peaceful, respectful lost land of content that was the 1950s.

This whole picture is, of course, utter claptrap. The idea that teachers are a seething horde of Bolshevik militants is palpable nonsense. The belief that schools up and down the country are ungovernable hotbeds of disaffection is ridiculous. The claim that more and more young people are leaving schools without any education is simply not true. Even the figures produced in official publications paint a very different picture to that present in newspapers and political speeches.

But if journalists and politicians are making wild and untrue claims for political advantage, it is nevertheless the case that large numbers of people, both teachers and parents, do think that there is something wrong with education in Britain. Indeed, in a capitalist society, especially one experiencing a long period of crisis, it would be very surprising if that were not the case. The political appeal of these scare stories is a good indication that there are real problems and real worries.[1]

The aim of this article is to try to outline what the issues underlying the press hysteria really are, and to show why they have arisen. In fact, as we shall see, although the Tories have made the problems very much worse during their long tenure in government, the origins of the crisis lie in the contradictory demands placed upon education in a capitalist society. Neither the plans of the Tory right nor the slightly less extreme views advanced by the Labour Party come anywhere near addressing the underlying problems. While a socialist solution is the only way that these can be solved, and a decent education for all assured, there are numerous smaller steps, that even a determined reformist government could undertake, which would go some way to improving the quality of education that working class children get.

Crisis? What crisis?

Whether or not there is a crisis in schools, and what its nature is, depends upon how one looks at the system. In a class society, of course, the viewpoints of the different classes give a quite different picture of society. For the ruling class, any crisis in public education is something in which they have no personal stake. While the state of schools may concern them as bosses, it does not worry them as people. Their children go to quite different schools, and face none of the same problems. For workers, on the other hand, any crisis is real and immediate. Working class children are the people who go through state schools, and it is their direct personal experience that is the first and best register of any crisis.

From the point of view of most teachers, and the majority of working class parents, the system is actually performing rather well in the narrow terms permitted it in a capitalist society. It might be shamefully failing to realise the potential of each and every child, and increasingly reduced to providing certificated fodder for the labour market, but it certainly meets those limited goals. That is to say, it is providing a higher level of educational qualifications than it was in the past. If there is a crisis, it is in terms of crumbling buildings, inadequate equipment and bulging classrooms, rather than poor results.

This is such a contentious claim that we need to look at the evidence. There are real difficulties in measuring the performance of any educational system over time, and it is certainly the case that educational outcomes, even in a capitalist society, are much wider than just examination results. Nevertheless, even if we accept the narrowest of definitions of success, official statistics seem to demonstrate that schools are doing a really good job. The crude measure of the number of qualifications gained by students at different levels of the education system show a clear rise, year after year.

It is difficult to measure these precisely, since there have been major changes in the examination system. Taking the situation for England alone, prior to 1988 the examination system in secondary schools was organised around 'O-levels' and 'A-levels'. These were both academic examinations designed to select pupils with the ability to pass examinations in order to ensure a supply of highly qualified entrants to a very restricted university system. A-levels were officially intended for the 'most able' 10 percent of students, and O-levels for 20 percent. In 1965 an additional examination was added, the CSE, which was designed for the next 40 percent of less academic pupils. In 1986 the system was reformed for the 16 year old age group. O-levels and CSE were abolished, and replaced by a new unified examination system called the GCSE, which came on stream in 1988. A-levels remained in place and continued to function as a major element in selection for higher education. There is no strict continuity between the two exam systems, but it is possible to compare the number of passes at O-level with the number of passes in the GCSE at Grades A to C and accept them as more or less equivalent measures of achievement.

TABLE 1: PROPORTION OF STUDENTS
WITH QUALIFICATIONS (ENGLAND)

Year	5 or more passes (O-level equivalent)	1 or more passes (O-level equivalent)
1974/75 (All school leavers)	22.6	81.1
1987/88 (All school leavers)	29.9	89.9
1988/89 (Pupils aged 15 at start of school year)	32.8	92.5
1994/95 (Pupils aged 15 at start of school year)	43.5	91.9

Despite the fact that the different methods of collection mean that the figures for the first two periods are relatively higher than they would be on a uniform measure, the evidence demonstrates very clearly that there has been a consistent and substantial rise in the number of students gaining some qualifications from their time in compulsory schooling.[2]

Although it remains an elitist examination, a similar picture emerges for A-levels, with more students doing better in these exams year after year. This trend shows every sign of continuing. In 1992-93, 30 percent of the age group had one or more A-levels and 19.2 percent had three or more. Two years later, in 1994-95, these figures had risen to 34 percent and 22.3 percent respectively.[3]

One of the objections put forward by Tories to a reliance on such figures as indicators of the fact that the education system is working quite well is the claim that numbers of qualifications have risen because examination standards have fallen. In the case of A-levels, there is no convincing evidence either to support or deny this charge over the long term. Both sides are reduced to swapping anecdotes based on comparing isolated examination questions and making claims for each as being more difficult than the other.[4] What we can say is that, while nothing certain can be known about the long term tendency, the fact that this trend is consistent even over the very short term of one year to the next, during which period there is very unlikely to have been any substantial change in the material taught, the quality of the teaching staff, the resources available, the preparation of the candidates, or the expectations of the examiners, suggests very strongly indeed that the rise in standards is a real one.

In fact, there was a recent scandal in which it was revealed that the A-level English candidates for one examination board, the Oxford and Cambridge, who were overwhelmingly from private schools, were systematically overmarked, because the examiners took more notice of the names of the schools than the answers actually produced. This, however, is likely to have been an exception, and the onus is on those who believe that there has in fact been a fall in standards to demonstrate how and when it took place, and how on earth it was kept secret. A plan to defraud the government and the public, involving thousands of teachers and hundreds of examiners working for different competing examination boards, agreeing clandestinely to relax examination standards little by little each year, would be a conspiracy of such scope as to make *The X-Files* and *Dark Skies* look like wholly believable documentaries.

All of these factors apply even more strongly in the case of the GCSE examinations, which have only been in place for a decade. Since, during that period, central control over what is taught and how it is assessed has in fact increased very considerably, without the government making any claim themselves to have relaxed standards, the probablity must be that the criteria have remained more or less the same, or even become more strict. It would require very strong evidence, rather than Tory prejudices, to establish that increasing examination success was the result of lower standards rather than increased achievement.

The rising rate of exam success, however, is only part of the story. Even when 40 percent of children leave school with good qualifications, there remain 60 percent who leave with little and 10 percent who have nothing in the way of certificates to show for their time in school. These young people, overwhelmingly working class males, seem to have been let down even by an ostensibly egalitarian comprehensive system and an inclusive, rather than selective, examination system. It is on the experiences of this group that a great deal of the professional and political discussion over a crisis in education focuses. One expert, who is both an Ofsted hitman and an adviser to Tony Blair, commented that:

> *While* [standards] *are rising for the many, they are low for perhaps 40 percent and perhaps falling for a significant minority of this group. In this failing group white working class males are predominant. It should be pointed out that, while standards have risen for advantaged, average and disadvantaged young people, they have risen faster for the already advantaged, while the rate of improvement amongst the disadvantaged is markedly slower.*[5]

The perception is that the effect of the current educational system is to recruit a substantial minority of working class males into an unskilled and effectively unemployable underclass which is the source of all sorts of undersirable and threatening social problems.

It is from this group of young people that those children excluded from school are mostly drawn, and that issue has focused very sharply popular concern with the education system. In fact, while the rate of exclusions from schools has risen sharply and, if the number of short term exclusions is counted as well, has reached a significant level, it remains a marginal problem for most schools. Even Ofsted, always determined to find the worst in schools, was forced to admit that when it went looking for trouble it found:

> *This survey...does not support the view that schools in general are degenerating into chaos. Most of the behaviour observed, even in poorly taught classes in inner urban schools, was at least satisfactory. Outside classrooms, an adult presence was usually all that was required to prevent serious misbehaviour. Most teachers dealt skilfully with potentially-challenging pupils. What appears to be happening is a degree of polarisation between the great majority of children who remain orderly and well-disposed and a small*

minority who are becoming increasingly intractable.[6]

The worry that confronts the more aspirational working class parent, who sees the education of their son or daughter as a golden bridge out of the working class, is that their child will find themselves in a school that has a large proportion of unsuccessful and potentially disruptive pupils, who will make it that much harder for their own child to do well. Since this group of aspirant workers is identified by pollsters as the crucial swing voters who make the key difference in elections, their worries and concerns are also the worries and concerns of politicians whose own children are assured of a very different educational experience.

Another group of working class parents have a different worry about the same phenomenon. Young Afro-Caribbean males are much over-represented amongst both those failing to achieve qualifications and those excluded from schools. In 1993-1994, for example, black Caribbean young people experienced 'almost six times the rate of exclusion for whites'.[7] The root of these grotesquely discriminatory outcomes is clearly the endemic racism of British society, although the precise mechanisms by which it operates remain much debated.[8] Despite this, however, these results can be seen as an extreme version of a much more common experience, shared by many white working class parents, particularly those in areas of high unemployment and social crisis.[9] They are evidence that the public education system is displaying increasing internal differentiation, with some schools giving up on some pupils, and some local authorities giving up on some schools.

The working class experience of education is thus contradictory. On the one hand, those students who get on all right at school, and who go to a school that manages to keep its head above water, have a good chance of at least moderate success. On the other hand, those who find school uncomfortable, or who find themselves in a school with problems, can face the prospect of having no qualifications in an increasingly certificated world.

The resulting worries about education can best be understood by analogy with the fear of violent crime. It is well known that the people who are most frightened of violent street crime, elderly people, are those least likely to suffer it, while groups like young males, who are much more likely victims, are very sanguine about it. Elderly people are more worried because they rightly perceive that they will be losers in any physical encounter, that the consequences of any injury will be much more serious and perhaps fatal, and that the loss of a purse or wallet will have a very great effect on their life. Young men, on the other hand, think, rightly or wrongly, that they can look after themselves, believe they are immortal, and that something will turn up to pay the bills.

In the case of education, most working class children will go through school without serious incident and leave with some qualifications. But the working class child who has difficulties is very likely to be discarded by the system and face a bleak future, and the working class community that sees its schools collapsing foresees a mass of consequent social problems. Even those working class people whose own experience of the system has been reasonably good know very well how fine a margin there is between success and failure, and how few of the resources of money and contacts that the middle and upper classes can call upon to help them overcome educational problems are available to them.

The politicians and upper educational servants of the ruling class have a different set of concerns altogether. They are worried about the relationship of the public educational system to the economy as a whole, and in particular the extent to which it is producing the right sort of labour power. For them, education is seen entirely in terms of providing 'opportunities on the labour market'.[10] Comparative educational research has identified some shortcomings in the achievements of British school students. Increasingly trapped in their own rhetoric of globalisation, politicians of all parties are worried by evidence that seems to suggest that other countries have education systems that produce better qualified young people. Agitation about this is focused on the mathematical and scientific abilities of school students, partly because this area, unlike the other key battleground of English, is one that lends itself much better to international comparisons, and partly because mathematical proficiency is identified, quite rightly, as the foundation of a range of skills needed in everything from banking to engineering. As the Chair of the School Curriculum and Assessment Authority put it, they are:

...actutely aware of the importance of mathematics in the school curriculum. Its role in preparing young people for the world of work is crucial in securing this country's competitive edge. We recognise that an increasing number of students are progressing to higher education, and that mathematical competence is required for them to benefit from many courses. And, at a basic level, participating in a complex, commercial and technological society calls on a range of mathematical skills. For all these reasons there is a need to improve the mathematical performance of all young people. Our country's position in international comparative performance tables leaves absolutely no room for complacency.[11]

In the view of the people running it, the overriding purpose of the education system, to which everything else must be subordinated, is international economic competition.[12] There is a pressing need radically to alter the way in which teaching takes place in British schools, in order to ensure that British capitalists can compete better on the world market.

Again the evidence is patchy and subject to a number of caveats, but a recent survey covering comparisons between England and the rest of the world suggested that:

- *Performance in science is rather better than in mathematics, but not appreciably so.*
- *Performance in mathematics in England is relatively poor overall...*
- *This performance deteriorated relative to other countries between the mid-1960s and the mid-1980s.*
- *Only at older ages in a highly selected system is English performance relatively good.*[13]

One of the key pieces of evidence adduced to support these views is the results of two sets of tests carried out on children in a wide range of countries. The first of these (First International Maths Study, or FIMS) was carried out in 1964, the second (Second International Maths Study, SIMS) was carried out in 1982. Students were tested at 13 and immediately before university entrance (in the UK usually 18). The first group was the general student population. The second was made up of mathematics specialists. The results for ten countries were compared amongst 13 year olds, and eight countries for the pre-university students.[14]

TABLE 2: RESULTS OF TESTS OF COMPARATIVE MATHEMATICAL ATTAINMENT

Test	Score Age 13	Rank Age 13	Score Age 18	Rank Age 18
FIMS	52.40	4/10	70.34	1/8
SIMS	44.23	9/10	65.00	2/8

Given that these scores are based on answers to the same set of questions at each point in time, they would appear to suggest both an absolute decline and a relative decline, at both age levels. Further evidence that this decline has continued since 1982 was found from the results of another comparative test (IAEPM2) carried out in 1990. This found that UK school students averaged 61 percent correct answers in a maths test, compared to 80 percent in China, 73 percent in Korea, and 73 percent in Taiwan. These figures are believed to lead to one obvious conclusion: that the high rates of economic growth in these Pacific Rim countries are a consequence of this mathematical achievement.

Anyone reaching this conclusion demonstrates an ignorance of social scientific methodology that should disqualify them permanently from serious discussion. They do not constitute evidence that there is any precise correlation between rates of economic growth and levels of mathematical achievement. They do not take into account the fact that the US, with lower scores than the UK on all measures, can be argued to have had higher growth rates. They do not demonstrate any kind of causal relationship between the two variables: there could be any number of other factors that explained the differences.[15] Indeed, they do not even demonstrate which way round the influence, if any, is.[16] On this evidence, one could as well claim that high rates of economic growth caused high mathematical achievement.[17] All the scores prove is that English (and in this instance, Scottish) students did less well in particular kind of maths tests than did those from a number of other countries, notably on the Pacific Rim, but also including Hungary and Switzerland.

What is more, this imaginary correlation is not perceived by the ruling classes of the countries in question. The education systems of the Pacific Rim, including Japan, are in turmoil, if not crisis. Although the local rulers believe that they have done quite a good job in the past in producing obedient and moderately skilled labour, they do not think the current set up is very good for the next phase of capitalist competition. They think that the schools and universities do not to produce enough of the 'creative professionals who will lead Asia's future economic growth', and are seeking to move away from the kind of training that the British elite find so admirable towards one that rewards greater initiative and flexibility.[18]

Whatever the truth, however, the relative educational decline of Britain, and consequent low rates of growth are widely believed to be both true and causally related, particularly by the upper educational professionals who are paid to think on behalf of the ruling class about these questions.[19] In so far as it has an opinion on these matters, the ruling class probably agrees, at least in its majority. Certainly, the CBI initiated a programme of targets for educational attainment that are now part of government strategy.

The basic reason for all the talk about a crisis in education is thus that political parties are exploiting the real worries of working class parents to attempt to gain support for changes to the education system that will fit it much more closely to what the capitalist class and its close servants believe is necessary for economic competition.[20] Achieving these ends, however, is fraught with difficulties that arise both from the contradictory nature of education in a capitalist society and from the peculiar way that it has evolved in this particular society.

Education in capitalist society

Like every other major institution in a capitalist society, the education system is structured by the basic dynamics of that society. Very crudely, education is one of the main mechanisms, alongside the family, whereby labour power is reproduced in society. The next generation of workers need to be prepared for the labour market in order for capitalism to continue to have the most important means of production, labour, at its disposal. Without that, in sufficient numbers and in the right condition, the task of producing surplus value is quite impossible.

Preparing the next generation of workers has two aspects. On the one hand, it is necessary to try to make a fundamentally irrational and unequal system appear sane and normal. On the other hand, it is necessary to impart the skills and attitudes necessary for the kinds of labour needed by capital. There is always a balance to be struck between these two goals.[21] For capitalism, it is important that people learn at school to be able to read, write, count and so on, but it is equally important that they learn to do what they are told and to submit willingly to authority.

That is not to say that schools exist only to teach young workers how to behave and that what is taught is completely irrelevant. That position is more or less exactly identical with the right wing 'functionalist' sociological explanation, which argues that the main purpose of education is to socialise young people into the norms and values of society and to minimise the possible social stresses arising from the allocation of positions within the division of labour. Against both left and right versions of this theory, Marxists argue that there is no central agreed value system in a class society. On the contrary, values are hotly contested. The key site of this contest is in the workplace generally, but the struggle undoubtedly spills over into all areas of social life, including the classroom.

Neither is it true that the education system is a direct expression of the needs of the system. In fact, different sections of the capitalist class need rather different kinds of labour. The drug companies need a smallish number of very highly skilled and innovative scientists, their technical support staff, and some moderately skilled production workers. Armaments manufacturers need a good number of qualified scientific and engineering staff and very highly skilled production workers of the traditional, metal working, type. Security companies need large numbers of young, fit, and preferably honest, men prepared to work extremely long hours for low pay. All of them need office and administrative staff. Banks and finance houses, on the other hand, need a few personable and sound young men with the right class connections, a number of mathematicians to build economic models, and a very large number of careful, and certainly honest, women capable of carrying out routine tasks involving computer mediated communication. In short, the capitalist class needs a wide variety of different kinds of labour.

It is the state, in its capacity as the executive committee of the ruling class, that is usually charged with resolving these competing demands. It, too, has its needs for labour: fit and obedient young people, mostly male, to carry out repression and aggression, and a minutely differentiated range of administrators to staff its civil bureaucracies. Achieving such contradictory ends can be very difficult. The capitalists themselves and their close servants are often quite mistaken as to what their real needs and interests are in education. The education system itself is a large social institution with its own ideas and values that does not just jump to attention at the latest DFEE circular. In addition, in a bourgeois democracy at least, the state has to negotiate with political parties that reflect, however inadequately, the interests of other classes. The resulting picture is usually one of a school system that pursues at least two different, and incompatible, functions. On the one hand, it educates the ruling class and its functionaries in the necessary social and technical skills for successful class rule.[22] On the other, it teaches the children of the working class the skills necessary for employment and the social attitudes necessary for a subordinate place in capitalism.

In advanced bourgeois democracies, these different ends are usually conducted within a single, comprehensive, system of education.[23] Both the USA and Japan, to name only the largest economies on earth, have fully comprehensive state education for the overwhelming majority of children. They have very small private sectors which cater for some sections of the ruling class and for members of various religious cults. While this may create difficulties in differentiating clearly between different social classes, it at least meets the formal criterion of bourgeois democratic equality.[24] Much of the debate in Britain, as we shall see, arises from the peculiar way in which these tensions are handled here. The purely functionalist account, whether in its left or right guises, does not really capture these kinds of problems.

While it is important to stress that the form of the educational experience, rather than the concrete content of what is taught and learnt, is vital to understanding education in a capitalist society, it is wrong to imagine that the content of what is taught is unimportant. Such a position comes close to accepting that meaning is arbitrary and truth meaningless. Once again, there is nothing particularly 'Marxist' about this: it is shared by sociologists like Pierre Bourdieu, and is obviously much developed in postmodern accounts of knowledge.[25]

The political danger is that it leads to an ultra-left rejection of education and knowledge on the grounds that it is 'all bourgeois ideology anyway'. The broad details of the Marxist response to this position are well known, even if the details are hotly contested. What we call 'culture' and 'science' are not arbitrary constructions. They are the historical products of human endeavour. Both are horribly distorted by the fact that they were produced in class societies, culture particularly so, but they nevertheless represent real human achievements. People in a future socialist society will still look at Velasquez's painting *Las Meninas* with love and fascination, even though they will live, think and feel in ways unimaginably remote from those distortions of humanity perpetrated by the Spanish absolutism that it represents. So, too, the working class movement today seeks positively to devour the culture and the science of all past and present societies in order to learn, to understand and thus to effect change. The conditions under which working class children get the chance to do that matter to us. We would prefer education to be secular, for example, to spare young people a struggle with the guilt perpetrated by religious ideology. If there must be religious education in schools, we are for it celebrating the great festivals of many religions, rather than unthinkingly reproducing Christian myths and thus unconsciously, or worse still consciously, denigrating other cultures. Similarly, we are for sex education and against any suggestion that anything other than married heterosexual relations are perverted. Anyone who really believes that the form of the educational experience is its central feature should, logically, be quite indifferent to such considerations of differences in content.

The view that content is unimportant is also wrong because it does not recognise that capitalist society needs a wide range of different kinds of skilled labour. It is true that all need to be obedient, but it is also true that the clerk needs certain kinds of skills, and that these are different from those needed by the electrician. Education plays a part in the development of these substantive skills as well, although a great deal of the actual training in particular jobs takes place in the workplace.

The major function of education, therefore, is indeed to prepare the next generation of wage workers. Much of what is involved in that process is precisely learning obedience and deference to authority figures. But a part of education is concerned with transmission of the social and technical skills needed to administer capitalist society. Part of what is taught to working class children is, potentially at least, valuable material that can be used to change the world. Above all, what actually goes on in education is not the direct result of what the ruling class wants. They, or at least their servants and agents, try to achieve that end, but they are challenged, more or less successfully, from below, by teachers, by parents and by young people themselves.

The Tories and education in Britain

The education system in Britain has a singular peculiarity compared with other advanced bourgeois democracies: alongside state provision for compulsory education, there has always been a very large private fee paying sector. By the early 1990s around 8 percent of all children were attending such schools. These schools are almost exclusively the preserve of those with large incomes. Eton College, the most famous of them, charges £12,888 per year for each child in its care. Winchester, the most academically successful boys' school, charges £13,290 for boarders and £9,966 for day students.

What these huge fees buy is academic success, and thus entry into elite universities. All upper sixth form students at Winchester pass at least three A-levels. Some 33 percent of Eton upper sixth formers pass four A-levels, and another 62 percent pass three. A full 98 percent of Winchester's upper sixth formers go on to university, 40 percent to Oxford or Cambridge. Only 86 percent of Eton's go on to university, 32 percent to Oxford or Cambridge.[26]

These are two exceptionally privileged schools, but there are hundreds of others that are in the same business in a more modest way. On average, the fees buy a better pupil/teacher ratio (10.8:1 in 1991) than do our taxes for state schools (18.8:1 in 1991).[27] These increased resources buy better examination results, both at GCSE and A-level:

TABLE 3: AVERAGE SCORES FOR A-LEVEL IN 1996
BY SCHOOL TYPE [28]

Type of school	Mean A-level score	Students scoring 30+
Comprehensive	14.8	10.8
LEA Grammar	19.9	19.3
LEA Other	9.4	2.2
Grant Maintained	17.0	14.7
Independent	22.1	26.7
VI Form College	15.4	10.8
FE College	15.9	13.2
Average all schools	15.9	13.2

'A-level' scores are computed by awarding each A-grade 10, B-grade 9, and so on, and totalling for each pupil, so a score of 30+ means three As or better. They are the basic standard measure used by university admissions officers to select students. Elite institutions demand higher scores than others. Overall just around half of the annual intake of undergraduates for Oxford and Cambridge comes from the fee-paying schools that educate less than one in ten of the age group. Since graduates of these two universities are disproportionately represented at the top of most professions and many industries, the very least that can be said about an expensive education is that it greatly improves a child's chances of becoming one of the close servants of the ruling class.

In other words, there is a structural divide in British education. The ruling class and its close allies have one kind of education. The working class get another kind. This division is even embedded in law. Working class children attend schools that are obliged to follow the National Curriculum. Ruling class children attend schools to which that set of prescriptions does not apply. The problem of trying to do contradictory things that faces state education in other capitalist countries is thus alleviated in Britain. It is in principle possible to ensure that the ruling class learns how to rule, while at the same time ensuring that the working class learns how to obey.

Unlike the case of the US, no one can pretend for a moment that British education is organised around egalitarian principles.[29] But a capitalist society, unlike feudalism, does not have closed and hereditary classes. There is no legal barrier to moving into and out of different social classes. A bourgeois democracy, moreover, finds it difficult to justify restricting entry to elite posts. Despite some very archaic features, British capitalism opened the civil service to competitive examination back in the 19th century.

Simply to tell workers that the best they and their descendants forever could look forward to was a life of toil and subordination would be greatly to encourage membership of a revolutionary socialist party. Much better to offer the chance of some improvement through success in the education system, particularly to the petty bourgeoisie and the upper layers of the working class. In addition, an expanding capitalism, forced to innovate and compete, needs to suck in all the talent it can get. It cannot rely on the fact that the children of the rich will have the skills and imagination needed to keep the system running.

The door to entry into the elite needs to be kept open, even if only a tiny crack. No one imagines that there is a British equivalent of the American dream, but there are some ways that working class children can find their way up the social ladder. One good example was the famous socialist playwright Dennis Potter, son of a miner in the Forest of Dean, but educated at Oxford. Another was the great socialist cultural theorist Raymond Williams, son of a Welsh railway worker, but educated at Cambridge. In both of these cases, their writing bears very strong and self conscious marks of that social journey. A character in one of Potter's plays repeats a little rhyme: 'I remember, I remember, the school where I was born'.[30]

In the 1944 Education Act, the need to keep this door open was enshrined in the very structure of the school system. The fee paying schools remained. In the English and Welsh public system, special schools, grammar schools, were consolidated, with the task of emulating the private sector.[31]

Entry into these schools was determined by the 11-plus examination. Those who did well went into little cesspits of provincial snobbery. All of the trappings of a private school—prefects, uniforms, cadet corps, rugby or hockey, and above all a highly academic programme including compulsory Latin—were built into the state sector and paid for out of taxes.[32] The aim was to permit the 'bright' boy or girl from the petty bourgeoisie or the working class to compete for a slightly higher position on the social ladder. The vast majority of the remainder of young people were judged to have 'failed' and sent off to secondary modern schools, where they got football and woodwork if boys, and cooking and sewing if girls, and a proper perspective on their future class position.

Not surprisingly, this setup was not popular, particularly with working class, and even petty bourgeois, parents, who resented the fact that their children were being written off at the age of 11. In the 1960s, the Labour government set about moving towards a comprehensive model of schooling, in which there would be no social sorting at the age of 11. This move was something of a shambles in practice, and resisted all along the line by some Tory ideologues, but nevertheless a clear majority of children were in comprehensive schools by the mid-1970s. Today, on one reliable measure, 79 percent of children are in such schools.[33]

The two big flies in this ointment were, first, that the reforms left the private sector untouched, and second, that there was no reform of the examination system. So long as A-level success remained the basic filter to university and thus to the higher reaches of the professions, this kind of academic success would be the common measure by which education, and thus any school, was judged. The private schools continued to do very well at getting children through such exams. A 'good' comprehensive was one that got the highest results in public examinations. A 'bad' school was one that got low results. Inside any comprehensive school, there would be a continual pressure to divert disproportionate resources to those children who showed the best chances of passing exams. Getting rid of grammar schools did very little to get rid of the social pressures that had made them what they were. Instead it reproduced the old divisions both between and within the new schools.

The same problems bedevilled two other important and related reforms. The first of these was a desire to end the internal ranking of children by academic performance through streaming them according to results. However socially desirable an end to selection inside the school might seem, and however much a logical consequence of the basic comprehensive idea, it was bound to fall foul of the drive towards competition and examination results. If such results were what mattered, then there would be a tendency to organise things so those with the best chances of success got the most energetic and able teachers, the best resources and the most school support. Such imbalances were bound to point towards streaming.

The second reform was a shift in the basic philosophy of what education was about. Many teachers came to hold the view, quite correctly, that each child had different abilities but that all were of equal worth. They also believed that education was not about filling a student full of facts and then testing them, but helping the young person to find out about, and understand, the world. This, obviously, is very close to what socialists want from education. Its implication was that what children were taught, and the way that they were taught it, had to shift.

The shift is best understood in the field of mathematics. In the old schools, whole classes of children learnt techniques (algorithms) for multiplying £17.4s.4¾d. by 47 $^{7}/_{16}$. This could be justified because the best that such children could hope for was to become clerks who needed such skills in their working lives. This changed. Children were now taught 'new maths', with particular emphasis on 'set theory'. The stress was no longer on instilling a set of routines into young minds without any examination of the underlying ideas. The aim of the new maths was to help children understand what they were doing. As one writer puts it:

...during the post-war economic boom, the social relations of education at all levels were developed in line with the economy's thirst for skilled white-collar labour to staff accelerating technological innovation. In accommodating to this process, much of the educational practice hitherto reserved for the professional and managerial elite was appropriated for these new layers who, far from being part of that elite, were actually destined to fill the increasingly large but relatively powerless middle levels of the industrial and service sectors.[34]

The dual effect of relaxed social conditions during the long post-war boom and pressure from the working class for more equal educational opportunities meant that some teachers were able to start teaching the sorts of things that were usually reserved for those picked out to help run society.[35]

Closely linked to this new content was a new idea of how children should be taught. The old philosophy was of a teacher standing at the front of a class, pumping ready made knowledge into the receptive young minds at a uniform and steady rate: 'a monster in a lecturing castle, with Heaven knows how many heads manipulated into one, taking childhood captive, and dragging it into gloomy statistical dens by the hair'. The new model, because it thought children should find things out for themselves and discover meanings rather than learn facts, involved a new way of teaching, focused on the needs and development of the individual.[36] This is called 'child centred learning', and again it has strong parallels with socialist views on education. Of course, to do it properly and respond to the actual learning process of each young person, teachers would need very small classes and lots of time, books and equipment.

Just as all of these good, if sometimes woolly, ideas were being put into practice, the economic and political system intervened. It is possible to name an individual and a year in which the attempt to turn back the clock began. The individual was not Margaret Thatcher and the year not 1979. Margaret Thatcher had in fact been education secretary during the Heath government, when the rate of comprehensivisation was highest and the progressive innovations in curriculum and pedagogy were coming into more general use. True, she had cut free school milk, but she had done nothing to halt the overall processes, nor even criticised them. In fact, the year was 1976, and the individual was James Callaghan, Labour prime minister. In a notorious speech at Ruskin College, he called for a 'Great Debate' on education. He said:

> I do not join those who paint a lurid picture of educational decline because I do not believe it is generally true, although there are examples which give cause for concern. I am raising a further question. It is this. In today's world higher standards are demanded than were required yesterday, and there are simply fewer jobs for those without skill. Therefore we demand more from our schools than did our grandparents.[37]

The Labour government was just in the process of launching a massive reduction in public spending in order to please the IMF, so Callaghan made it very clear that one solution was absolutely unthinkable: there would be no more money to solve any problems the debate revealed. What is striking about this speech—indeed 20 years later it is quite shocking—is the extent to which it presages the exact ideas and themes of current Tory demagogues. Here, unquestionably, we have a Labour government preparing the way for the Tories.

In the event, the Great Debate was derailed by the class struggle and achieved little in the way of real change. When Thatcher came to power, she too had more pressing problems like steel workers, and then miners, to attend to, and education was mostly neglected in the early years. Although the Tories did not much like what was going on in the state schools, they had not yet either the plan or the political will to carry through any major changes.

Contrary to popular rumour, the Tory governments have not slashed spending on education. It is true that expenditure as a percentage of Gross Domestic Product (GDP) fell from 5.1 percent in 1979-80 to a low of 4.6 percent in 1989-90, although it has since risen to 5.1 percent again.[38] In international terms this is low, but not remarkably so. In 1993, when it stood at 5.3 percent of GDP, it was lower than other EU member states, but not dramatically lower than another state with an ageing population like Germany, which spent 5.4 percent.[39] In absolute terms, spending has been rising, since the relatively constant share of GDP has been a proportion of a growing total. If we look a little more closely at the figures for recent years, however, we find an interesting shift:

TABLE 4: TOTAL EDUCATIONAL EXPENDITURE IN ENGLAND[40]
(CONSTANT 1994-95 PRICES)

	1979	1990/91	1991/92	1992/93	1993/94	1994/95
Current	14,795	14,747	15,524	16,189	16,116	16,590
Capital	963	881	841	825	890	913
Total	15,758	15,628	16,365	17,014	17,006	17,503
Cap/Tot	6.1%	5.6%	5.1%	4.8%	5.2%	5.2%

It is obvious that, while total educational expenditure has risen in recent years, and has been above 1979 at least since 1991-92, capital spending has not yet recovered to its earlier figure, and has consistently been a smaller part of the total than previously. Given that the figure for 1979 was itself depressed by previous Labour cuts, this must be one of the main reasons for the fact that, as every parent and teacher will tell you, the buildings in British schools are in a shocking state. Although the drop is not that great, two decades of marginal underfunding have the cumulative effect of a major disaster.

There are two other very important things that need to be said about the figures for expenditure. First of all, they are for all education and training expenditure. Since both the training and the higher education sectors have expanded during the years of Tory rule, schools have not accounted for all of this rise in real spending. If one removes all of the money that has gone into various training programmes, and into the vastly expanded higher education sector, then the increase for schools is much more modest.

A second major factor has acted to distort the impact of the small real increase and to make it appear much larger than it really has been. The number of children, and the number of schools, has fallen dramatically over the last decade. Between 1979 and 1991 the number of pupils enrolled in state schools fell from 8,242,837 to 6,635,396, a fall of 19.5 percent.[41] This contraction has allowed the Tories to claim that, despite static or only slightly rising total expenditure, there has been a sharp rise in spending per child: they claim a real term rise of 55 percent per child in primary schools and 49 percent in secondary schools.[42]

Because of these falling numbers of students, although there was a fall in the number of teachers employed in the state sector from 245,981 in 1980 to 194,428 in 1993, there was no comparable rise in class sizes.[43] In fact, class size in England remained more or less constant. In primary schools it rose from an average of 26 in 1980-81 to 27 in 1992-93, and in secondary schools it fell from 22 to 21 over the same period.[44] While in primary schools the number of very small classes of less than 20 pupils with one teacher fell from 20 to 10 percent, the number of very large classes, with more than 31 pupils per teacher also fell, but only from 22 to 20 percent of the total. A similar, but less extreme, picture operated in secondary schools. The increase in resources per student did not therefore mean that classes got smaller overall. The number of very small and small classes fell, as did the number of very large classes. There was much greater uniformity of class size, with most being of the quite large 21 to 30 size. The fact that one in five classes still has more than 30 students in it is evidence that the Tories have not provided adequate educational resources. Teacher input per student is by far the most important aspect of education. Only with small classes can a teacher give real attention to the needs of each individual student. This aspect of education has barely changed during Tory rule. At the same time, as we shall see, there have been numerous changes that have increased the burden on teachers. The net effect is that teachers now have classes of roughly the same size as they had 20 years ago, but face an enormous mountain of additional duties and responsibilities. Thus, while it is true that the Tories did not worsen education resources in absolute terms, their claims to have improved them are spurious.

Tory policy on education cannot be dismissed simply as an attempt to justify cuts. If it were that simple, there would be a simple, if scarcely credible, reformist answer to all problems: pressure the next Labour government to spend a bit more on schools. Reality is much more complex and much more intractable. What Tory policy has really done is to intensify pressures on the schools that would anyway have been present because of the logic of capitalism, and which have been magnified by the instability of the economy.

What the Tories have tried to do is to bring the education system much more into line with what they perceive to be the social and political needs of society. In order to do this, they have attempted to push the system back as far as possible to the state it was in before the start of comprehensivisation. That is to say, they have attempted to separate out as clearly as possible the aspect of schooling designed to educate the ruling class and its upper servants from that aimed at preparing the future proletariat for the world of wage labour. In carrying these policies through, they have not been entirely consistent, partly because they have contradictory perceptions of what is needed by capital, partly because they are trapped in their own general ideology, and partly because of political realities.

The latter, for example, has meant that it has not been possible simply to reinstate full blown grammar schools. There are no doubt many in the rank and file of the Tory party who would like to do this, but the idea remains sufficiently unpopular even with many Tory supporters as to be impossible to implement: what happens to Darren if he fails the 11-plus? What they have tried to do is to create an intermediate zone between the private sector and the comprehensive sector that has an impact much greater than the numbers of children it affects.

The Tories, of course, had no problem with the private sector: most of them were educated in it, after all. It is completely consistent with their hostility to social provision, and their desire to roll back the state, to encourage people to pay for services like education. The 1980s and 1990s have been a golden era for private schools.

The trend of declining enrolments was reversed. Despite the occasional problem caused by recession, the number of pupils in fee paying schools rose from 512,233 in 1979 to 546,156 in 1991. At the same time as the overall school population was falling by 19.7 percent, the number of fee payers rose by 6.6 percent.[45] As a proportion of total school students, private pupils rose from just under 6 percent to around 8 percent.

The first step they took on the road to increasing differentiation in the state sector was to introduce an 'Assisted Places Scheme' that paid the fees of a few, academically selected, children to go to private schools. The costs of the scheme are considerable, and have risen much faster than the general education budget. In 1985-1986 this scheme cost £30 million; by 1994-1995 it cost £101 million.[46] One major effect of this scheme is thus a considerable subsidy to the running costs of private schools paid out of taxation. It was, however, presented as a method of broadening access to private education. As the 1980 Education Act claimed, it was a scheme 'for enabling pupils who might not otherwise be able to do so to benefit from education at independent schools'.[47] The Tories, and the private school system, like to present this an opportunity for bright but poor children from inner city areas to experience the benefits of an expensive education. According to the most detailed analysis of the scheme: 'It was justified as an extension of parental choice, a restoration of academic opportunities to any able children whose local comprehensive schools were inadequate, and as essential protection for those individuals and for the nation's resources of talent against the levelling down effects attributed to the demise of so many maintained grammar schools.'[48] When we look at who has made use of this scheme, however, it becomes clear that the main beneficiaries are the upper reaches of the middle class.

The scheme bases its assessment on income, not wealth, and so blatantly have the realities been disguised by some parents that, in interviews with researchers, many headmasters of private schools admitted they were very suspicious of some of the claims made by parents. Even accepting the limits of the selection procedure, however, it is clear that the scheme is not benefitting the children of the working class: 'Less than 10 percent of these pupils had fathers who were manual workers, compared with 50 percent with fathers in service-class [relatively privileged middle class—CS] occupations, while almost all the employed mothers were in white-collar employment'.[49]

One striking feature of beneficiaries is the number that come from single parent families. Forty percent of assisted place families were headed by a single parent, while the national figure was 4 percent of all families. Almost all of these families were headed by a woman.[50] This startling generosity on the part of a government that is more commonly associated with vicious attacks on single mothers is put in perspective when we understand the class of mother in question here: '...evidence indicates that 68 percent of mothers of assisted place pupils, and 51 percent of fathers, had received an education that was either private or selective.'[51]

Not to put too fine a point on it, the main function of the Assisted Places Scheme has been to make sure that young Philippa and Rory can still get a good education, even though Daddy has run off with his secretary, or been downsized rather brutally, or both together.

The second major element in Tory policy was the introduction of the possibility of schools 'opting out' of local authority control into grant maintained status. The aim was to create a state financed sector of education which, unlike the comprehensives, would ape the private sector:

The government envisages that the policy of 'freeing' schools from the constraints of LEA control will help them to become better managed and more responsive to the needs of parents who 'will enjoy enhanced influence over their conduct' (Tory minister Angela Rumbold in 1989). In addition, it is argued that opting out will foster healthy competition between all schools, including those in the private sector. It is claimed that such competition will lead to a general improvement in educational 'standards' and break down the barrier between public and private provision. GM schools, in other words, will become a 'half way house' between state and independent schools, ending the existing unfairness of a system in which 'only the wealthy have choice' (Norman Tebbit in 1987).[52]

In practice, persuading schools, and the parents who must vote for this measure, actually to opt out has proved rather difficult, and the government has made every effort to push up the numbers. As one measure, the government has offered explicit bribes.[53] By 1995 GM schools accounted for 5.6 percent of the total but got 14.1 percent of the capital spending, 2.7 times as much on average as an LEA school.[54] Despite these bribes, by January 1993 only 337 schools had opted out, 255 of them secondary schools. The government have displayed great determination to raise this number, and the policy has gone through a range of versions in an attempt to make it more attractive.[55]

One particular angle they have worked ceaselessly is the claim that opting out is a response to parental desires to escape from the incompetent and levelling policies of Labour led local authorities, who have been pursuing an ideologically driven agenda at the expense of parents and children. The evidence does not bear this out. In 1993 only 13 percent of opted out schools were in Labour areas and around two thirds were in Conservative led authorities. London and the south east, together with the east Midlands, both key places where the Tories won the votes of aspirant workers, were heavy areas of transfer.[56] In fact, what GM status has done is to provide a way in which that minority of parents who want their children to have an expensive education, but who don't have the money to pay for one, have been able to obtain a (very) cheap imitation.

The third area of policy arises directly from the above. The introduction of a National Curriculum, applied to all state schools, and the development of testing for all children (SATs) were designed to pit school against school. This introduction of competition into an area previously considered a public service fitted Tory ideology very well, of course, since they think that this is the way to make British capitalism more efficient and internationally competitive. It has an additional benefit that it allows much greater control over what is taught and how teachers work in the classroom.

If a good school is one that does well at examinations, then the publication of regular league tables of examination results would permit everyone to see which were the best, and which the worst schools in an area. The basic comprehensive idea, that all schools should aim to provide an education for a whole range of students, the academically able and those whose abilities lie in other directions, was thus undermined. Certain kinds of academic achievement were now defined as the central measure of a school's success. The distorting effect of an elite public examination, that had always been present as a result of A-levels, was now to be extended down to children aged seven, and soon, perhaps, even five.

The logical corollary of this policy was that schools would select pupils. Although the rhetoric is one of parental choice, in reality 'good' schools are invariably oversubscribed and therefore have to exercise some form of discrimination between potential pupils. Both sides of this choice equation are deeply marked by class. One study of the ways in which parents made decisions demonstrated that the ability to make use of the published material required the parents themselves to have certain quite developed intellectual skills:

> *Although school examination results were felt to be useful by about half of the parents, many felt that they were difficult to understand. A written description might be a useful addition for those parents who have difficulty under-standing statistical information.*[57]

From the schools' point of view, an NUT study of the effect of testing six and seven year olds showed that younger children, those from poor backgrounds and those from ethnic minorities were likely to score less well. The temptation for schools to select out such pupils would be strong.[58]

It is not hard to see the further consequences either. In the pursuit of examination results, there must be a pressure to stream children by their perceived abilities. Back in 1990, when the tests were still fairly new, two commentators wrote:

> *Given that so much depends on them, the proposals to publish school average scores or grades will encourage schools to use whatever devices they can to raise those averages. Already there is some evidence that schools might well perceive that the best way to maximise their overall test scores is to stream by achievement level. Such an approach has attractions for those who take seri-ously the notion of hierarchies of attainment. Indeed, if one is prepared to accept that there is an invariant sequence of learning attached to a particular topic, it does seem somewhat unlikely that pupils will progress at exactly the same rate and in exactly the same way. Within such a philosophy, streaming **does** work: it produces hierarchies which reproduce themselves. Children in top streams **do** fare better than those in bottom streams—so streaming pro-vides its own self-justification.*[59]

Success, esteem and resources will flow to those children who can drag up the school score. Persecution is likely to be the lot of those seen to be disrupting progress.

It is this factor that has led to the sharp rise in exclusions. In a strik-ingly revealing phrase, Ofsted commented that permanent exclusion 'was seen less as a sanction than as an act of self defence by the school'.[60] Defence against what? It might be that a very small number of young people are a physical threat to teachers and fellow students, but they are best handled by therapies designed to reintegrate them with normal social life. These, of course, are expensive and time consuming. The real worry, surely, is that the effect of diverting resources to such efforts, and the disruptions that might ensue, would lead to worse test scores. It is much easier, and certainly very much cheaper, for the school to refuse to teach children with these difficulties. The children are victims of an attempt by the schools to defend themselves against failing in the tests.

All of these measures, taken together, amount to a massive attempt to ensure that testing and selection, and thus the grooming of an elite, become one of the organising principles of the school system. They have the added advantage, from the Tories' point of view, of taking the understandable worries of working class parents, and their hopes for the future of their children, and trying to channel them in a reactionary direction. What is more, unlike the old grammar school setup, there is no huge visible barrier that acts to screen out most working class children, and which it is almost impossible to cross at a later date.[61] The process of selection works under the cover of alleged market competition.

There is, however, another side to the Tory plan. We saw that educating an elite is only one part of the role of education in a capitalist society. The other side of the coin is to prepare the future proletariat. The Tories have pursued this aim with some vigour too. One of the goals of the introduction of competition into the school system was to try to do this more effectively without increasing the resources. The Tories have altered the content of education too. Not only is 'enterprise' now an official part of education, but there is a new emphasis to vocational training, and those parts of academic education like the sciences, that can be claimed to be directly related to 'wealth creation'. Between 1985-1986 and 1991-1992, the number of pupils in vocational education in the UK rose by 31 percent. In the EU this figure was only exceeded by Greece (36 percent) and Spain (37 percent), while in Germany, which is so often taken as the model for vocational education, it actually fell by 22 percent.[62] While the Tories have maintained the A-level as the 'gold standard' determining university entrance, they have also created a battery of new qualifications, NVQs and GNVQs. The 'Vs' stand for vocational, and it is unconvincingly claimed that these are to have equal status with academic qualifications.

The third function of education that the Tories are trying to enhance is the disciplinary aspect. Teaching people to know their place, to behave properly, not to question the existing order, and so on, is the meaning that lies behind the talk of a need for more moral education in schools. This has nothing to do with developing children's talents and abilities, or their capacity for relating to their fellow human beings. It is entirely about imposing upon them a set of beliefs that lead them to obey. It is here that the analysis of capitalist education as a purely formal means of disciplining the future labour force is at its strongest.

In sum, then, one could say that the Tories have attempted to do three distinct things with British schools, which all correspond to different needs experienced by British capitalism. They have attempted to maintain the private school system, and strengthened it by means of state subsidy. This is designed to provide an education for the ruling class and its future upper servants. They have created a new layer of schools, the grant maintained sector, that is better funded than other state institutions, that is highly oriented towards examination success defined in nearly the same terms as the private sector. This sector is designed to provide a few entrants to the upper reaches of the class system, and to train the large number of technical specialists needed a little lower down. To support this, they have introduced the regular publication of test results for all publicly funded schools, so that the ranking of different schools according to their academic success is apparent to everyone. Finally, they have tried to tighten up on the displinary aspects of all public education, and in particular that in the local authority run part, by introducing a national curriculum instructing teachers what to teach and increasingly attempting to change the content of education and the manner of its delivery to reinforce this. The aim of this policy is to produce docile proletarians ready for exploitation.

Why it hasn't worked

Of course, in practice things have not turned out this neatly. If the Tories' plans had all gone through smoothly, if they had correctly identified the needs of capitalism and devised policies to meet them, and if they had not met resistance from other classes, then there would be no crisis in education. Everybody, or at least the vast majority, who were on track to become members of the ruling class and its servants would be delighted. Everybody or nearly everybody who was destined to become a middle ranking expert would be contented. Everybody, or at least many, who had been brainwashed into thinking that all they were fitted for was to follow orders would be resigned to their fate. There might be occasional mutterings, but not this deep sense of crisis, and no reason for the continuing political agitation.

There are at least three reasons for the failure. The first is to do with the difficulty of planning in a capitalist economy. Because capitalism is a constantly changing system, and because the balance between different branches of economic activity, and indeed the geographical location of whole industries, is determined by competition rather than reason, it is very difficult for any government to have a clear and consistent idea of what is needed. The needs of capital today are not necessarily the needs it will have tomorrow, and the production of new labour power necessarily has a long lead time. There is nothing, as yet at least, that is available in the way of technology to speed up the rate of human maturation.

In the case of Britain in the 1980s, this general problem was exacerbated by the fact that the pattern of employment was changing very rapidly, both between industries and in terms of the gender balance:

TABLE 5: PERCENTATGE OF EMPLOYEES BY INDUSTRY AND GENDER[63]

	MALE				FEMALE			
	1971	81	91	94	1971	81	91	94
Agriculture	2	2	2	2	1	1	1	1
Energy & Water	5	5	3	2	2	1	1	1
Manufacturing	41	35	29	28	29	19	13	12
Construction	8	8	7	6	1	1	1	1
Distribution	13	15	19	20	23	24	25	24
Transport	10	9	9	9	3	3	3	3
Finance etc	5	7	11	13	7	9	13	13
Other service	15	18	20	21	35	41	44	45

These changes should not be interpreted simply as a shift from 'manual' to 'white collar' occupations, since many of the jobs in distribution and other services are themselves manual working class jobs. However, inside manufacturing itself there was indeed such a shift. In 1985, 26.3 percent of manufacturing workers were classified as 'adminstrative, technical and clerical', but by 1992 the figure was 34.2 percent.[64] Overall what these figures do show is that there were big changes in the kinds of jobs workers were doing during this period, and therefore in the kinds of skills that were needed.

Planning an education system that fitted at all precisely to these kinds of changes, and at the same time satisfying the quite contradictory demands for labour of different parts of the capitalist class proved quite impossible. The Thatcher governments were, notoriously, indifferent to manufacturing and saw the future in finance capital and services. Since then, there has been something of a new sensitivity to the needs of industrial capital, and this explains some of the recent stress on the need to produce labour that fits the needs of an internationally competitive manufacturing industry. The shifts and lurches, however, only serve to emphasise how impossible it is to plan labour in a capitalist economy.

This difficulty is exacerbated in a bourgeois democracy by the fact that it is very difficult to direct young people into certain kinds of employment. Even quite young children are very far from being the passive recipients of an educational experience determined by others. As they get older, children exercise choice within an education system, and a competitive society has an ideological investment in allowing them to do so, at least up to a point. In British society, one of the consequences of this choice has been that children who do well at school have tended to prioritise the academic over the vocational, and the humanistic over the technical. It is notorious that university departments offering 'flakey' and 'non-serious' subjects like media studies are much harder to get into than those offering solid, production oriented things like engineering.

The other side of this coin is that children who are not academically able make such decisions as well. In the 1970s a classic study by Paul Willis showed how young working class male children made a definite choice to put their energies into acquiring the cultural habits of manual workers, rather than the much more middle class ones that the schools offered them.[65] What is often vulgarised as the influence of role models on young people is much more a question of them making assessments of the kinds of futures open to them, and the kinds of rewards and indignities each will involve. One of the consequences of the new stress upon examination success is that more and more children have their noses rubbed into the fact that the system regards them as second rate and fit only for ruthless exploitation. Not surprisingly then, the choice of a non-academic future becomes increasingly attractive, and with it an increasing disaffection with school. One study found that 10 percent of children aged 14 to 16 were regularly illicitly absent from school, 50 percent claimed not to like school, and 20 percent described themselves as actively unhappy there.[66] It is this perfectly understandable adaptation to official rejection that leads to the long tale of educational 'failure', the lack of qualifications and, in a minority of cases, to the kinds of behaviour that result in actual exclusion.

The third reason for the problems faced by the Tory policies is that they contradict each other. It is all very well to analyse the competing needs of different sections of capital and to try to translate those into a need for different kinds of education, it is quite another to find a way of implementing them in practice. The kinds of things that are learnt, and the ways that they are taught, are quite different in an education aimed at producing the rulers of a society and that aimed at producing its subordinates. Keeping the two distinct in any school system is almost impossible, although the existence of private schools makes it easier in Britain than in some other countries.

One clear example comes from mathematics. The National

Curriculum reduced the range of mathematics taught in schools, and shifted the emphasis within it. Systematic testing ensured that teachers would follow the syllabus rigidly in order to have well prepared candidates. But the nature of the curriculum is not necessarily directly suited to all of the expectations placed upon it. Multiplication and long division were once a central part of the mathematics curriculum. There were, arguably, good economic reasons why these were needed in production—although in practice most people would use ready reckoners for financial calculations and log tables and slide rules if they were scientists or engineers. They then more or less disappeared, as part of the move towards new maths teaching, and their place in doing those sort of sums was increasingly taken by the calculator. The time and energy released were devoted to aspects of mathematics that were seen as much more intellectual and that might lead to a better understanding of the nature of mathematical thinking. The kinds of mathematical education appropriate to the higher servants of the ruling class seeped down into other classes with different destinies. The introduction of the National Curriculum reversed this trend:

> *The recent battles with various UK government agencies which resulted in the downplaying of 'using and applying' mathematics and the introduction of long division algorithms illustrates nicely that those in power do **not** believe that mathematical knowledge is politically neutral. At the rhetorical level, the debate was about downplaying an area of mathematics seen (by both sides) as potentially enlivening mathematical creativity. On the other hand, the introduction of long division represented an attempt to impose on the curriculum a piece of mathematical knowledge which is both anachronistic and* **use***-less. At precisely that point in the evolution of human knowledge when knowledge of how to divide a three digit number by a two digit number becomes redundant, the government of the UK passes a legal requirement to teach it to all pupils (other than the privately educated).[67]*

The only value to learning such skills is that, in experiencing the routinised and mind numbing discipline involved, young people will learn that they have to follow orders, no matter how pointless they may seem. While this might seem to be an important part of the education of the future proletariat, it is certainly not something that the ruling class needs, and it is not really the optimal education for their higher specialists. In the existing system, however, it is what everybody subjected to the National Curriculum will get, no matter what their future class position.[68]

A similar set of contradictions marks the problem of how children are to be taught in schools. Probably no teacher anywhere, except possibly the most doctrinaire, uses entirely one method or another, but it is obvious that child centred techniques go together with a concern to develop the individual's knowledge and understanding. This fits well with the educational goals of the ruling class, or at least of its upper servants, who need to understand at least some things about capitalist society. But in state schools producing future workers, it would be likely to encourage working class children to get ideas above their station, particularly if the school had the resources in terms of teachers and facilities to do it properly. As a consequence, this method of education is under attack, in favour of 'whole class' methods. These have the advantage of being cheaper and more conducive to a passive learning experience based on the unquestioning acquisition of received knowledge.

Once again we can see this process at its clearest in the teaching of mathematics. Studies of methods of teaching in countries with higher maths scores, notably those of the Pacific Rim and Switzerland, stress that in these countries there is much greater emphasis on 'whole class' teaching. However, the same observers also note that the use of 'child centred' teaching in Britain leads to 'a substantially greater cumulative increase in variability as children pass through the school than in mainland Europe'.[69] In other words, what the existing methods do is to help the mathematically able child do well in exams. What is more, it is claimed that the condition for the success of the Pacific Rim countries is partly to do with the absence of competition within at least the primary classroom. The results are based on 'the use of mixed ability classes in the early years of school, with all children receiving basic skills in an egalitarian setting, and learning to value the importance of the group and of co-operation.'[70]

Within capitalist relations, at least, there seems to be a choice. An educational system built around whole class teaching of mixed ability groups of children who learn to work with, rather than against, each other produces a fairly homogenous level of mathematical achievement. This is not only ideologically unpalatable but difficult to achieve in a system that is in every other respect finely calibrated to produce a range of differentiated achievement from the very highest through to the functionally innumerate.

What Tory policies have ultimately foundered upon is the contradictory demands placed upon them by the capitalist economy. Funding decisions have played a part: whatever the Tories say about the increases they have made, they have not been enough to meet the needs of teachers and students. Ideology has played a part: some aspects of what they want are frankly not in the interests of any class at all. The attempt to win political support from sections of ambitious workers has played a part: some children have been given the chance to do well at the expense of others. The underlying problem, however, is that, in an unstable but viciously hierarchical system like capitalism, it is just not possible to produce an education system that both satisfies all the economic needs of the system and does not provoke massive social discontent.

Conclusions

These problems have been present in the system for at least 20 years, as the similarity of rhetoric between James Callaghan and his Tory successors demonstrates. What has exacerbated them in the 1990s is the effect of the economic crisis. Although the Tories can publish statistical papers until they are blue in the face showing beyond question how much more is now spent on education than in the past, the common perception is quite the reverse: teachers and parents firmly believe that the system is starved of resources and struggling to survive. The reason for this is that the strains and pressures on everyone in the system have been increased enormously.

The business of systematic testing is massively time consuming in itself. The social crisis outside the schools has a direct effect in the classroom. Not only does it mean that teenagers are difficult to persuade of the value of education but it also means that more and more children are coming into the schools with difficult social circumstances.[71]

This leads to huge increases in pressure on the time and energy of teachers and others. The institution of the National Curriculum, not to mention the incessant attacks on teachers in the Tory press, leads to demoralisation. The replacement of properly qualified inspectors by the kangaroo court of Ofsted, with its slapdash inquisitions, ten minute assessments of classes, and brief to find the worst it can, has immeasurably increased the stress on teachers. One index of the fact that teachers are tired, overworked and fed up is their desire to get out of the job. The recent decision to stop teachers taking early retirement was the government's response to this. In 1979-1980, 7 percent of male teachers between 50 and 59 took early retirement and 9.5 percent of female teachers took the same decision. By 1992-1993, the figures were 23.8 percent and 22.3 percent respectively.[72]

The Labour Party propose to do almost nothing about this. Needless to say, they have no intention of getting rid of the private school system. It is true that they have said they will abolish the Assisted Places Scheme, once the current beneficiaries have enjoyed their subsidy. That is to be welcomed. They do not, however, propose to wind up grant maintained schools: indeed, they send their children to them. In fact, what they propose to do is to rename them foundation schools and put them under some local authority control, but they will still 'have an opportunity to develop...the ethos which many GM schools feel they have developed'.[73] The have no plans to abolish, or even reform, the National Curriculum. They have no plans to abolish the SATs. They have said that they will introduce compulsory homework—even for primary school children.[74] They even intend to keep the appalling Chris Woodhead on as head of Ofsted. Frankly, they are not going to solve any of the problems and have no intention even of trying.

In fact, any serious reformist government could do quite a lot to improve education, even without having to spend any additional money, and certainly without threatening capitalism as a system. Abolishing private education and grant maintained schools would simply bring Britain into line with such hotbeds of radicalism as the US—even former Tory minister George Waldon is in favour of that move. The National Curriculum, with its restrictions over teachers' freedom to respond to the particular needs of different groups of children, could be dropped without a lapse into savagery. Above all, getting rid of SATs and transforming Ofsted into a supportive body would take a lot of the pressure off schools.[75] With some more money, even a little, much could be done by way of trying to provide the resources that would enable class sizes to be reduced and child centred learning to be developed.

A socialist education policy, of course, would be something else entirely. We can't explore it in any detail here, partly for reasons of space but mostly because it is ludicrous for the products of a semi-barbarous society to try to guess how the free human beings of a future civilised society will order their affairs. We can, however, try to guess its outlines. We can predict that it is likely to be comprehensive, humanistic, and based on educational discovery by the pupil. In this, it will be the exact opposite of any existing system.

A socialist system will be comprehensive because it will value the full range of human activities as being of equal worth. It will not privilege one particular kind of ability, that of passing theoretical examinations, and claim that this is the highest end of education. It most certainly will not use that sort of criterion as a passport to a better rewarded, easier and longer life.

It will be humanistic because it will seek to develop the unique combinations of talents and abilities that are to be found in any human being. Its aim will not be to fit people into a niche in the class structure, or to equip them for profitable exploitation in their working lives. On the contrary, it will be an end in itself, part of the very business of living in the world.

Finally, it will seek to explain the world. Its aim will not be to fill children full of facts and ready made interpretations. It will be organised to help people find things out, to understand their world, to discover new things, and to modify what is already known in the light of their interests and experience.

Some of these aims are to be found, in whole or in part, in the best elements of education in a bourgeois society. We are unequivocally for the defence of such advances, and of the people who try to implement them under impossible conditions. But in the end we seek their universalisation—and that is possible only in a different sort of society.

Notes

1   I should make clear what the scope of this article is. Scotland and Northern Ireland have different educational systems to England. Wales has one that is much more similar but still significantly different. Most of the arguments and facts in this article apply to the English system. I have noted when that is not the case. These other systems have some of the same problems and some of their own, but I don't have the space to look at them here.

There is another problem that is specific to readers outside of Britain. There is a whole special language of hypocrisy about education in Britain. We do not mean the same thing as Americans when we say 'a public school'. We actually mean a private school. An 'independent school' is another euphemism for one run on the basis of fees. I have tried to use terms that will not confuse people. When I talk about public education, I mean education provided by the state, either national or local, and funded out of taxes. I have called other schools either private or fee paying.

2   Government Statistical Service, *Statistics of Education: Public Examinations GCSE and GCE in England, 1995* (HMSO, 1996), p9.

3   Department for Education and Employment, *Statistical Bulletin: GCSE and GCE A/AS Examination Results, 1994/95*, No 6/96 (HMSO, May 1996), p31.

4   In order to make any serious claim, it would be necessary to administer the same test to two groups of students and compare the results. History being what it is, this means that it would be necessary to give a test from the 1960s to contemporary students and to have them marked by the same markers, then compare the results in detail. This is impossible for three reasons. Firstly, the content of the syllabus has changed over time, so the current students would be disadvantaged compared to the historical group. Secondly, even if the same examiners are still alive and available, they would now be much different people, and we would have no guarantee they were making the same judgements. Thirdly, for quite understandable reasons, nobody bothered to keep the examination scripts of my 30 year old A-level in Pure Mathematics, and I am absolutely certain that I could not repeat the performance now. The historical evidence necessary to such a comparison simply does not exist.

5   M Barber, *The Learning Game* (Gollancz, 1996), p27.

6   Her Majesty's Chief Inspector of Schools, *Exclusions from Secondary Schools 1995/6* (HMSO, 1996), p29.

7   D Gilborn and C Gipps, *Recent Research on the Achievements of Ethnic Minority Pupils* (Ofsted, 1996), p52.

8   The evidence is patchy and contradictory, but it seems that there is something much more complex than 'crude' racism based on skin colour at work. It is well known that African-Caribbean girls do much better than African-Caribbean boys, and in fact do better than white boys. It also seems to be the case that African boys do better than white boys and much better than African-Caribbean boys, while African girls do slightly less well than the other two groups of young women. One

study in Lambeth in 1994 found the following average exam scores by ethnic origin and gender:

	Male	Female
African	21.9	26.5
Caribbean	15.1	26.6
'White'	19.8	27.5

[Source: ibid, p28]

These results should be treated with some caution. The sample was small, and geographically limited in scope. There appears to have been no control for social class or any other demographic variables.

9   One study, now slightly dated, found that in London, once the analysis was extended to a more complex range of demographic factors than simply ethnicity, social class emerged as a major determinant of success: 'This research is consistent with previous work finding that, in 1987, the examination results of fifth year students of Bangledeshi, Caribbean and Turkish origin were significantly below those of other groups. After taking into account the students' sex in each of the 14 ethnic groups studied, and their VR band on entry to secondary school, together with the characteristics of the schools attended, it was found that students of Caribbean, and of English, Scottish and Welsh origin were performing least well. This suggests that these findings have as much to do with social class and expectations...as they do with ethnicity.' 'Foreword by the educational officer' in ILEA Research and Statistics Branch, *Differences in Examination Performance*, RS 1277/90 (ILEA, 1990).

10   H Steedman and A Green, *Widening Participation in Further Education and Training: A Survey of the Issues* (Further Education Funding Council, 1996), p4.

11   N Tate, 'Opening Remarks' in *Conference Proceedings. SCAA invitations Conference: Mathematics for 16-19 Year Olds* (London, 11 December 1995), p5.

12   This, incidentally, is an extremely clear example of what Marx called the 'fetishism of commodities', whereby real human relations appear only in so far as they exist to produce commodities for the market: 'The two-fold social character of the labour of the individual appears to him, when reflected in his brain, only under those forms which are impressed upon that labour in everyday practice by the exchange of products. In this way, the character that his own labour possesses of being socially useful takes the form of the condition, that the product must be not only useful, but useful for others, and the social character that his particular labour has of being the equal of all other particular kinds of labour, takes the form that all the physically different articles that are the products of labour, have one common quality, namely, that of having value.' K Marx, *Capital*, Vol 1 (Progress, 1965) pp73-74.

13   D Reynolds and S Farrell, *Worlds Apart? A Review of International Surveys of Educational Achievements Involving England* (Ofsted, 1996).

14   Ibid, p9.

15   These are called intervening variables, in the jargon.

16   They have failed to identifiy the independent variable, in the jargon.

17   The logical error is vividly illustrated by another possible conclusion that the authors don't, of course, draw. The political systems in these countries range from the recently imperfectly democratised (Korea and Taiwan) to the brutally repressive (China). On their logic, one would be inclined to conclude (1) that mathematical achievement leads to political repression and (2) that the greater the mathematical achievement the higher the level of repression.

18   'Asian Education: Devalued Diplomas' in *Far Eastern Economic Review*, 14 November 1996, p24.

19   What is more, they think that these good exam results contribute to the social
      peace that they believe prevails in these countries. They really should read
      newspaper reports about South Korea a little more carefully.
20   To call this a 'utilitarian' approach to education would be to insult the memories
      of Bentham and the Mills. They, after all, believed that the proper aim of social
      organisation was to maximise human happiness. The vulgar views peddled today
      seek only to maximise profitability.
21   The most influential statement of the basic Marxist case was by two US writers,
      Bowles and Gintis. They argued that, while it is one function of the educational
      system to legitimise economic inequality, it is much more centrally concerned
      with producing the right kind of workers: 'Reference to the educational system's
      legitimation function does not take us far toward enlightenment. For the formal,
      objective and cognitively oriented aspects of schooling capture only a fragment of
      the day-to-day social relationship of the educational encounter. To approach an
      answer, we must consider schools in the light of the social relationships of
      economic life...we suggest that major aspects of educational organisation
      replicate the relationships of dominance and subordination in the economic
      sphere. The correspondence between the social relation of schooling and work
      accounts for the ability of the educational system to produce an amenable and
      fragmented workforce. The experience of schooling, and not merely the content of
      formal learning, is central to this process.' S Bowles and H Gintis, Schooling in
      Capitalist America (Routledge, 1976), p125. Because they were writing about the
      US, where the education system is predominantly public and comprehensive, they
      were forced to argue that the legitimation function of education was the result of
      its apparently meritocratic character: 'The educational system legitimises
      economic inequality by providing an open, objective, and ostensibly meritocratic
      mechanism for assigning individuals to unequal economic positions. The
      educational system fosters and reinforces the belief that economic success
      depends essentially on the possession of technical and cognitive skills—skills
      which it is organised to provide in an efficient, equitable and unbiased manner on
      the basis of meritocratic principle' (ibid, p103). For obvious reasons, discussed
      below, no one would ever imagine that British system had a similar meritocratic
      structure. There are some overall problems with this position, as reformist critics
      have been quick to point out. For example S Aronowitz and H Giroux, Education
      Still Under Siege (Bergin and Carvey 1993). Rather more sympathetic, but still
      very critical, is R Brosio, A Radical Democratic Critique of Capitalist Education
      (Peter Lang, 1994). In later works Bowles and Gintis modified their position to
      take account of some of the contradictory aspects of capitalist education.
22   Strictly speaking, members of the capitalist class do not need to be educated: their
      social position derives entirely from their ownership of property, not their personal
      accomplishments. They can always hire someone with an education to run the
      business. As was remarked long ago, 'The capitalist mode of production has
      brought matters to a point where the work of supervision, entirely divorced from
      the ownership of capital, is always readily obtainable. It has, therefore, come to be
      useless for the capitalist to perform it himself. An orchestra conductor need not
      own the instruments of his orchestra, nor is it within the scope of his duties as
      conductor to have anything to do with the "wages" of the other musicians...
      Inasmuch as the capitalists' work does not originate in the purely capitalistic
      process of production, and hence does not cease on its own when capital ceases;
      inasmuch as it does not confine itself solely to the function of exploiting the
      labour of others; inasmuch as it therefore originates from the social form of the
      labour process, from combination and co-operation of many in pursuance of a
      common result, it is just as independent of capital as that form itself as soon as it

has burst its capitalistic shell.' K Marx, *Capital*, Vol 3 (Moscow, 1971), pp386-387.

23 For a good survey of just how widespread the comprehensive system of education is internationally, and a clear picture of just how odd British concerns are in this context, see C Benn and C Chitty, *Thirty Years On: Is Comprehensive Education Alive and Well or Struggling to Survive?* (London, 1996), pp15-22.

24 In fact, although both systems are very different, they tend to make their primary social selection at the same time: the point of university entrance. Both the US and Japan have very clearly graded university systems, success in the competitive entry to which goes a long way towards determining a young person's future. Kimiko and Tatsuro both go to the same school and learn the same things, but their parents pay for them to attend private cramming night schools to get them through exams. Then Tatsuro goes off to Tokyo (or Keio, or Waseda) while Kimiko goes to the local two year Woman's College. So too with Harvard (or Stanford, or Columbia) and the Middle Tennessee State University.

25 See, for example, P Bourdieu and J C Passeron, *Reproduction in Education, Society and Culture* (London, 1977). For Bourdieu, the dominant culture of any society is essentially an arbitrary construction whose value lies only in its differentiation from the culture of subordinate classes. Schools attempt to impose this dominant culture as the norm through the exercise of symbolic violence.

26 All these figures, and a host of others about even the most obscure fee paying school, can be found on *The Times* worldwide web site (http://www.the-times.com/).

27 Department of Education and Science, *Statistics for Schools in England, 1991* (HMSO, 1992), p133.

28 Department for Education and Employment, op cit, p21.

29 In fairness, it should be said that some other advanced capitalist countries, including the US, do have a tiny private sector primarily for parts of the ruling class itself and partly for various religious groups.

30 Although I have quoted two people who came out of it all as socialists, the vast majority of the people who followed this road adapted to the ideas of their new social position and became apologists for capitalism.

31 The Scottish system was, and is, rather different. Space forbids a full discussion here, but it has tended to produce the same general outcomes as its southern cousin.

32 About the only good thing that can be said for the grammar schools is that they taught a minority of their working class pupils undying class hatred.

33 C Benn and C Chitty, op cit, p88.

34 R Noss, 'Sets, Lies and Stereotypes', in S Lerman (ed) *Cultural Perspectives on the Mathematics Classroom* (Dordrecht, 1994) p41.

35 Noss goes on to say: 'The rhetoric of modern mathematics was—in the UK at least—rather straightforward. At root, it hinged on the idea that the display of mathematics as a formal system, unified by the ideas of sets, would allow pupils to see mathematics as a coherent whole, offer a greater degree of involvement and understanding, and result in a more substantial fraction of pupils studying mathematics at post-school levels.' Ibid.

36 The official recognition of this new approach was the Plowden Report, set up by a Tory government but reporting in 1967. Plowden argued that a child brought up in a school which 'lays special stress on individual discovery, on first hand experience and on opportunities for creative work...has some hope of becoming a balanced and mature adult and of being able to live in, to contribute to, and to look critically at the society of which he forms a part.' Cited in R Noss, 'Structure and Ideology in the Mathematics Curriculum' in *For the Learning of Mathematics*, 14(1), February 1994, p8.

37   Quoted in Barber, op cit, pp33-34.
38   DFEE, *Statistical Bulletin: Education and Training Expenditure since 1979/80*, Issue No 5/96, May 1996 (DFEE), p13.
39   European Commission, *Key Data on Education in the European Union* (Office of Official Publications of the EU, 1995), p56.
40   DFEE, *Statistical Bulletin: Education and Training Expenditure since 1979/80*, No 5/96, May 1996 (DFEE), p12.
41   DES, *Statistics of Education 1991* (HMSO, 1992), pp200-201.
42   DFEE, op cit, p16.
43   DFEE, *Statistics of Education: Teachers, England and Wales, 1993* (HMSO, 1996), p14.
44   Central Statistical Office, *Social Trends, 1995 Edition* (HMSO, 1995), p49.
45   DES (1991), op cit, pp200-201.
46   DFEE (1996), op cit, p6.
47   Cited in T Edwards, T Fitz and G Whittey, *The State and Private Education: An Evaluation of the Assisted Places Scheme* (The Falmer Press, 1989), p1.
48   Ibid, p1.
49   Ibid, p161.
50   Ibid, p165.
51   Ibid, p169.
52   T Fitz, D Halpin and S Power, *Grant Maintained Schools: Education in the Market Place* (Kogan Page, 1993), pp75-76.
53   John Major put it very frankly in a letter to the NUT in August 1991: 'We have made no secret of the fact that grant maintained schools get preferential treatment in allocating grants to capital expenditure. We look favourably at GM schools to encourage the growth of that sector and I am delighted to see that numbers are growing rapidly.' Cited in T Fitz, D Halpin and S Power, op cit, p30.
54   Labour Party, *Diversity and Excellence: A New Partnership for Schools* (Labour Party, 1995), p10.
55   T Fitz, D Halpin and S Power, op cit, p30 argue that: 'The government's resolve to drive opting out forward, despite the manifest difficulties associated with its implementation, is explained in large measure by the compatibility between the policy's central features and the ideological and political commitments of successive Conservative administrations. In particular, opting out simultaneously offers the prospect of increasing choice in education and satisfying groups within society whose support the Conservatives wish to attract and retain. For these reasons, education ministers have been prepared to adjust and amend the details of opting out and, ultimately, to promote it as the flagship of educational reform.'
56   Ibid, p40.
57   A West, et al, *Choosing a Secondary School: The Parents' and Pupils' Stories*, Clare Market Papers No 7 (LSE, 1993), p57.
58   'In one sense, this differentiated performance by various groups of children should not be so significant in a criterion referenced assessment system. Children are not being judged against each other, they are being assessed against certain statements of attainment in a more absolute way. In an ideal world, all will be given the opportunity to attain more with time. However, in a situation where schools appear to be in the position of being judged by the outcomes of the assessment, such ideals may have little relevance. Under these circumstances, younger children in a year group, children from poorer social backgrounds, children for whom English is a second language and children with special educational needs seem to be a distinct liability on a school roll. There is likely to be a tendency for some schools to regard such children as less welcome if 'raw' assessment outcomes remain the basis for comparison. At the same time girls, children who

have had nursery experience and the opportunity to teach children in smaller classes are each likely to be regarded as an asset.' NUT, *Testing and Assessing 6 and 7 Year Olds: Final Report* (with the University of Leeds School of Education), (NUT, 1993), pp56-57.

59   H Goldstein and R Noss, 'Against the Stream' in *Forum for the Discussion of New Trends in Education*, Vol 33(1) (NUT, 1990), p5.

60   Her Majesty's Chief Inspector of Schools, op cit (1996), p29.

61   Actually, the 11-plus still exists untroubled in Northern Ireland.

62   Eurostat, *Education Across the European Union, Statistics and Indicators* (Office of Official Publications of the EU, 1995), pp296-297.

63   Central Statistical Office, *Social Trends, 1995 Edition* (HMSO, 1995), p68.

64   Central Statistical Office, *Annual Abstract of Statistics, 1995 Edition* (HMSO, 1995), p108.

65   P Willis, *Learning to Labour: How Working Class Kids Get Working Class Jobs* (Gower, 1997). Willis's research problem was...: 'The difficult thing to explain about how middle class kids get middle class jobs is why others let them. The difficult thing to explain about working class kids is why they let themselves' (p1). He answered it by showing that: 'We can say that for a good proportion, the disaffected—in relation to whom the conformist case can be better understood—this is in the form of a partial cultural penetration of their own real conditions and a mystified celebration of manual work which nevertheless preserves something of a collective, rational, though incomplete, logic' (p185). It is striking how 20 years ago this book was written against the background of the fact that: 'there is currently a "crisis" in education' (p189).

66   M Barber, op cit, p84. Barber is big moral discipline man.

67   R Noss, op cit, p45.

68   Of course, things are a little more complex and a little more contradictory than I have made them appear here. The drive to insist on the possession of these redundant skills, as useful to the modern economy as the ability to translate Latin, is part of a more generalised ideological offensive which includes even the education of the ruling class and their close servants. There is currently a bitter row, involving threats of writs, between the School Curriculum and Assessment Authority and its expert mathematical advisers. The SCAA consulted mathematical opinion about whether to insist on part of the examination for AS and A-level being undertaken without calculators, but: 'The SCAA's report admits that only a "minority were in favour of the proposal to require AS and A-level candidates to take at least one paper without the support of a calculator" and that "only a quarter of consultees considered that the proposed 25 percent of marks for non-calculator papers were appropriate". Despite this, SCAA reaffirmed that "an element of assessment worth at least 25 percent of the marks and in which no calculator may be used has been retained". P Baty, 'Legal Threat Hots up Maths Syllabus Row' in *The Times Higher Education Supplement*, 10 January 1997, p2. While ideologies in general correspond to the aims of particular classes, ideologists systematise them even at the expense of what might be functional (this is another reason why functionalist explanations won't do). In this case, mad ideologists are insisting that even those people who are most likely to become mathematicians and scientists learn these obsolete skills. The time to learn these will have to be found in a curriculum that already drives some mathematicians to despair because it contains no consideration of the concept of mathematical proof.

69   S Prais, 'Improving School Mathematics in Practice', in *Proceedings of a Seminar on Mathematics Education*, London 27 February 1995 (Gatsby Educational Foundation, 1996), p7.

70   D Reynolds and S Farrell, op cit, p55.

71   For example, the number of pupils in public sector schools with statements of
      special educational needs rose from 38,200 in 1985-1986 to 86,900 in 1991-1992.
      Department for Education and Employment, *Education Statistics for the UK, 1993
      Edition* (HMSO, 1994), p47.

72   Department for Education and Employment, *Statistics of Education: Teachers in
      England and Wales, 1993* (HMSO, 1996), pp20-21.

73   Labour Party, op cit, p15.

74   And they have made some threatening noises which suggest that they quite like
      the idea of changing higher education so that an elite get three years at University
      and the rest get only two, for which they will have to pay, of course.

75   There might be an educational rationale for an agreement between a pupil, the
      parents and a teacher that that individual's educational development would be well
      served by testing how much they had absorbed by a certain point in time. But this
      is completely different from a compulsory standard national test of all students
      whose results are then aggregated by school and published. As a matter of fact,
      even the government's own committee that set the SATs in motion did not push
      for the raw results to be published. It wrote that, even in those countries that had
      national tests, 'publication of test results of use outside the school is virtually non-
      existent, except in some states of the US. There results have been published with
      adjustments for socio-economic background'. Task Group, *National Curriculum
      Task Group on Assessment and Teaching: A Report* (DFEE 1988), p12. British
      results, of course, are unadjusted.

The politics of information technology

COLIN WILSON

The last few years have seen an extraordinary wave of enthusiasm for computers, particularly for the internet computer network. In Britain nearly a third of households have a computer. Computers are advertised as vital to children's education. They appear in films from *Jurassic Park* to *Goldeneye*. And this, we are told, is only the beginning. Computer company Olivetti states that over the next 20 years computers will be involved in almost every aspect of people's daily lives, from controlling laser guided vacuum cleaners to replacing visits to the doctor: 'You may never have to go to a doctor again. You could simply have a tele-conference with your physician, using sensors to transmit vital information.'[1] Bill Gates, multi-billionaire head of the software company Microsoft, predicts that a computer will soon be available so small that it can fit into a pocket:

> It will display messages and schedules and also let you read and send electronic mail and faxes, monitor weather and stock reports, and play both simple and sophisticated games. At a meeting you might take notes, check your appointments, browse information if you're bored, or choose from among thousands of easy-to-call-up photos of your kids.

The tiny computer will also take the place of money and of keys, and give appropriate traffic reports.[2]

It is not surprising that computer companies make great claims for their products but such claims are widely accepted. Most Americans, for example, believe that by 2000 cars will have computer controlled navigation systems, and that computer technology will mean you can watch any TV show you want at any time—and that by 2005 cash will be obsolete and home appliances will respond to spoken commands.[3] Indeed, no statement about the importance of computers seems too extreme. The blurb for one academic study of the internet, for example, begins as follows:

> *Multimedia, the information superhighway and the internet have changed our world almost beyond recognition. Electronic networks have revolutionised the human relationship to time and space, and have undermined national boundaries.*[4]

Politicians of both the right and left accept the idea that computers are changing all our lives fundamentally. Deputy Prime Minister Michael Heseltine has claimed that society is:

> *...about to go through a revolution which is immensely exciting, basically a technological revolution of the superhighways... People today have not fully grasped the effect it's going to have on their lives, but it is, in my view, of incalculable consequence... People will have more leisure and will have more wealth...it's all very exciting, very positive.*[5]

The Labour Party's information technology policy also asserts that large scale social change is on the way:

> *New technologies...will bring fundamental change to all our lives.*

> *The ways in which we do business, or study, or receive broadcast entertainment, or receive healthcare, or shop, or make use of public services, will be transformed in a host of innovative ways.*[6]

These large social changes have, of course, political consequences. Theorists of all political colours agree that we are going through an 'information revolution'. Just as the industrial revolution fundamentally changed the world to bring about modern industrial society, so the information revolution will create a new, information society. For the right, all this is a triumphant vindication of capitalism. Technology is constantly advancing, bringing more and more advanced technology with no increase in price. Computers will assist in creating what Bill Gates describes as 'friction-free capitalism':

> *Capitalism, demonstrably the greatest of the constructed economic systems,*

has in the past decade clearly proved its advantages over the alternative systems. The information highway will magnify these advantages. It will allow those who produce goods to see, a lot more efficiently than ever before, what buyers want, and will allow potential consumers to buy those goods more effectively. Adam Smith would be pleased. More importantly, consumers everywhere will reap the benefits.[7]

Computers can even, apparently, solve capitalism's social problems. On his second day as speaker of the US House of Representatives, right-wing Republican Newt Gingrich proposed that poor people, including the homeless, should be given tax credits so that they could buy a computer and so increase their skills and chances of employment.[8]

On the left most analysis of information technology starts from a wider 'post-Fordist' view of society, such as that put forward by *Marxism Today* in the 1980s, based on the claim that we are living in 'New Times':

Unless the Left can come to terms with these New Times, it must live on the sidelines... At the heart of New Times is the shift from the old mass-production Fordist economy to a new, more flexible, post-Fordist order based on computers, information technology and robotics. But New Times are about much more than economic change. Our world is being remade. Mass production, the mass consumer, the big city, big-brother state, the sprawling housing estate and the nation-state are in decline...[9]

The world has been changed so thoroughly by information technology, the argument runs, that we no longer live in the kind of industrial society established in Europe in the last century. It follows that a political theory like Marxism, which set out to analyse and change that society, no longer applies in the modern world. Marxism might, at best, have had something to say about a world of cotton mills and coal miners—but how can it hope to respond to the internet or to the work of computer programmers? Marxism is outdated and this is nowhere clearer than in the field of information technology.

Writers associated with this journal have repeatedly confronted the ideas of post-Fordism and it is not my intention here to rehearse those general arguments.[10] Rather, I want to examine the claim that information technology in particular is beyond the reach of Marxist analysis. To what extent have computers fundamentally changed the world? Is the computer industry really different from the capitalist industries of earlier periods? Is Marxism capable of understanding the technologically advanced world of the late 20th century, and of forming useful political strategies based on that understanding?

Have computers changed all our lives?

The expansion of the computer industry in the last 50 years has indeed been enormous. In 1947 one computer engineer predicted that six computers were all the United States would ever need.[11] In fact by 1994 there were some 82 million computers in the US and 200 million in the world as a whole.[12] Making computers, and the chips that control them, has become a major industry. For many white collar workers in the developed world computers have become as integral a part of their office equipment as phones or photocopiers. The trend is set to continue, with the world market for personal computers reportedly growing at 30 percent a year.[13] Communications between computers is one of the areas of fastest growth—the numbers of computers connected to the worldwide internet computer network, for example, currently doubles about once every 12 months.[14]

As well as becoming more numerous, computers have become more accessible. The first computers were enormous machines which filled whole rooms, impossible to use without highly specialised knowledge. In the 1960s and 1970s computers became a little more widespread but they were still physically huge and extremely expensive by today's standards. These machines often needed to be installed in special rooms, and contact with them was only possible via an elite of programmers and administrators. In the early 1980s this changed dramatically with the introduction of small machines such as the IBM Personal Computer— ancestor of most personal computers in use today—and the Apple Macintosh, selling for a few thousand dollars. As machines have become smaller and cheaper they have also become more powerful, and this means that they can run software which is much easier to use.

There is, then, a real basis to claims about the 'information revolution.' But for all this, information technology is available to a tiny minority of the world's population. Most people in the world still have homes without electricity. According to the Labour Party's 'information superhighway' policy, 'half the people in the world have never made a phone call'.[15] Figures for the availability of telephones are worth looking at in more detail, since most people outside universities and large companies who access the internet do so over phone lines. The figures for the numbers of 'internet hosts'—large computers connected to the system— make much the same point as those for the availability of phones.

Only some 20 countries—such as the US, Japan and the European Union states—really have access to these technologies. In others, such as the Pacific 'Tigers', Eastern Europe or Latin America, some access is available. But in the African and Asian countries, where most people in

PHONES AND INTERNET HOSTS BY COUNTRY [16]

Developed countries	Phones per 1,000 population	Internet hosts
Australia	481	309,562
Belgium	469	30,535
Denmark	869	51,827
Germany	545	452,997
Italy	440	73,364
Japan	512	269,327
UK	519	451,750
USA	483	6,053,402

Pacific 'Tigers'		
Hong Kong	541	17,693
Singapore	388	22,769
South Korea	294	29,306
Taiwan	366	25,273

Eastern Europe		
Poland	93	24,945
Romania	99	954
Russia	163	14,320

Latin America		
Brazil	62	20,113
Chile	55	9,027
Mexico	70	13,787

Africa and Asia		
Angola	4	0
Bangladesh	2	0
China	9	2,146
Congo	7	0
Egypt	10	591
Ghana	2	6
India	5	788
Kenya	9	17
Morocco	10	234
Pakistan	'about 7…'	17

the world live, telephones are a rarity—let alone computers and the internet. The exclusion of Africa and Asia from new technologies has been typical of capitalism for a century—in 1912, for example, 67 percent of the telephones in the world were in the United States, 26 percent in Europe, 1.3 percent in Asia and 0.3 percent in Africa.[17]

Access to information technology is denied not only to many countries but to many people in the richest countries. Some 43 percent of Americans have never used a computer, and only 31 percent of the population own one.[18] An estimated 15.7 million people in the US had access to the internet by the end of 1996—only some 7 percent of the population, in the country with more computers than any other. Computer use is dominated by the middle class. Fully half of American internet users, according to one survey, have household incomes of over $50,000.[19] Another survey of users of the world wide web (www), one of the most popular services on the internet, found that:

●*25 percent of www users earn household income of more than $80,000 whereas only 10 percent of the total US and Canadian population has that level of income.*
●*50 percent of www users consider themselves to be in professional or managerial occupations. In contrast, 27 percent of the total US and Canadian population categorise themselves as having such positions.*
●*64 percent of www users have at least college degrees while the US and Canadian national level is 29 percent.*[20]

Class is not the only factor influencing people's use of computers. While 57 percent of Americans have used a computer, for example, only 16 percent of retired people have done so.[21] Men are twice as likely as women to use the world wide web, and this reflects the sexism prevalent in all areas of computing.[22] However, class is the most important factor in the simple sense that most people cannot afford a computer. When people who did not own computers were asked why they did not buy one, 72 percent replied that it was because they cost too much. Asked if they would learn how to use a computer if they received one as a gift, 92 percent of people who didn't use computers replied that they would.[23]

Computers are increasingly used as an educational resource—the best selling encyclopaedia in the world, for example, is Microsoft's *Encarta* software. Microsoft claim that *Encarta* sells five times as many copies as the best selling printed encyclopaedia, at a fraction of the price.[24] However, such resources are in practice available only to those children whose parents can afford a computer. Children without computers at home have to rely on schools to provide them—and government figures show that there is only one computer for every 18 children in British primary schools, and one for every ten children in secondary schools. Over half of the computers included in these figures are over six years old and, as such, probably obsolete. So in practice one modern computer is available per class.

The Labour Party, if elected to government, 'would hope to persuade companies to donate or sponsor equipment'.[25] One of the highlights of Labour's 1995 conference was Tony Blair's announcement of a deal with British Telecom; in return for access to the lucrative video-on-demand market, BT would cable up every school. But there is no chance that business would donate the millions of computers necessary to give every child access to one. Even if every school were connected to computer networks for free, they would still need funding for the phone calls they would make along their new cabling when connecting to computer systems. Teachers would still need training. Labour's proposals would not change the basic position that very few working class children have proper access to computers.

Altogether, far from breaking from a society based on class, in which the developing countries have little access to technology, and workers in the developed world have far less access than the middle class, computers continue these trends inherent within capitalism. Indeed at every stage of their development computers have reflected the capitalist society that gave them birth, and the inability of the market to meet people's needs.

The history of computers, the market and the state

The general principle that computer technology can only be understood in the context of capitalism, and that the market prevents the full development of that technology, goes back even to the 19th century prehistory of computers, when Charles Babbage attempted to develop his 'Difference Engine' and 'Analytical Engine'. The roots of Babbage's work lay in the political development of France after the revolution of 1789, and the economic development of Britain after industrialisation. It was probably in 1819, aged 28, that Babbage travelled to Paris and saw the mathematical tables of de Prony, which were to have an enormous influence on him. De Prony had been commissioned during the Republic to prepare an immense set of mathematical tables to celebrate the metric system, and by implication the rational nature of the new political order. The tables were the largest ever conceived and it seemed at first that they would be impossible to complete since too few people were available to do the required calculations inside a lifetime. However, de Prony chanced on a copy of Adam Smith's *The Wealth of Nations*. Smith argues that the division of labour is central to efficient manufacturing.

He gives the example of a pin factory—if one person carries out all the operations involved in making a pin, he argues, the factory is much less productive than when each operation is assigned to a separate worker and one rolls out the wire, another cuts it, and so forth. De Prony based the production of his tables on such a 'division of labour'. He assembled three groups: the first included six of the best mathematicians in France, and they set out the overall plan for the project and the general form of the calculations to be used. These formulae were then handed to the second group, consisting of seven or eight competent mathematicians who transformed the general formulae into calculations involving actual numbers. These they handed on in turn to the third group, formed of 60 to 80 people, most of whom knew no more mathematics than addition and subtraction. The third group worked out the calculations which the second group had given them, and in this way the tables were completed. De Prony had shown that intellectual work could be automated like any other sort of work.[26]

The creation of mathematical tables was an important issue for British capitalism in the early 19th century. The development of commerce and banking made necessary millions of calculations. In the absence of any kind of calculator, people either worked these out in their heads, or referred to sets of tables. In particular, the development of British trade with the rest of the world made accurate navigational tables vital. However, there were inaccuracies in all the existing tables. This meant that ships were wrecked, and financial affairs miscalculated. Babbage asserted, for example, that the British government had lost between £2 and £3 million because of errors in tables used to calculate annuities.[27] Babbage planned to build a machine—the Difference Engine—which would produce tables automatically, with no possibility of error, and in 1823 he received funding from the government to do so.[28] Over the next 11 years, the government was to spend over £17,000 on the Difference Engine project—by far the largest government sponsored research project of the time. Part of the Difference Engine was completed and worked perfectly, but the whole machine was never made (it would have consisted of over 25,000 metal parts, and weighed several tons).[29] In the 1840s Babbage began theoretical work on an Analytical Engine, which he continued to develop on paper until his death in 1871. Though consisting of metal parts, the Analytical Engine shares many features with modern computers. Punched cards were to be used to input data and programs—a technology borrowed from the Jacquard loom, where punched cards controlled the patterns woven into the cloth. In the words of Ada Lovelace, a collaborator of Babbage's and one of the first people to write computer programs, 'The Analytical Engine *weaves algebraic patterns* just as the Jacquard-loom weaves flowers and leaves.'[30]

As well as his work on the Difference Engine, Babbage wrote widely about the development of capitalism in Britain. He campaigned unsuccessfully for the reform of scientific education, arguing that the state must support scientific research if Britain's economy was not to fall behind those of countries with more interventionist governments, such as that of Germany.[31] Babbage's experience demonstrates two aspects of the development of technology under capitalism. Firstly, capitalism has made possible technological advances which would have been unimaginable previously, as Marx and Engels noted in 1848 in the *Manifesto of the Communist Party*.[32] Babbage's own work is testimony to capitalism's technological vigour—that he attempted, with some success, to build machines resembling computers at a time when the most complicated mechanism most people had ever seen was a clock.

But Babbage's work also demonstrates that the market cannot respond adequately to the potential for new technology which capitalism creates. However much Babbage's machines would have increased the profitability of British capitalism as a whole, there was never any question of his work being funded by industrialists who could make massively greater profits in the short term from textiles and railways. In the absence of such funding he looked to the state.

Conservative politicians have argued for 20 years that the state must have a minimal role in the economy if it is to thrive. Nationalised industries have been sold off so as to shed the supposed dead weight of state bureaucracy, emerging as efficient and profitable competitors in the market. Such ideas have now been accepted by some on the left—Tony Blair's rewriting of Clause Four of the Labour Party's constitution, for example, involved rejecting a commitment to nationalisation and replacing it with a formulation which accepted the 'dynamism of the market.' However, the idea that the state has only the most minor role to play in the economy squares very badly with history. The development of capitalism saw major change in the nature of the state in every country—including revolution in Britain and France. Legal systems expanded massively to provide the necessary framework for business, including contracts, patents and copyrights. Permanent armed forces were created. State intervention in the economy took place at a local and national level—local government in Manchester, for example, was strongly committed to free trade and the development of capitalism, but by 1905 the local state had invested £7.4 million in water, £2.6 million in gas, £2.3 million in electricity supply, £2 million in tramways, and £5 million in building the Manchester Ship Canal.[33] National governments worldwide intervened in the development of railways—as Eric Hobsbawm comments:

Without exception the new railway systems were planned by governments

*and, if not actually built by them, encouraged by the grant of favourable con-
cessions and the guarantee of investments. Indeed, to this day Britain is the
only country whose railway system was built entirely by risk bearing and
profit making private enterprise...*[34]

Babbage's work thus reflects three elements of capitalism: the enormous acceleration of technological development; the inability of the
market to harness that development; and the intervention of the state in
support of the new technologies. These three elements have characterised
the history of information technology from Babbage's time to our own.

The birth of computing

Far from stimulating further work, Babbage's ideas fell into obscurity
until the mid-20th century, after the invention of the computer at the end
of the Second World War, when various machines were developed in
reponse to the needs of the military. In Britain a machine called the
Colossus was designed to decipher coded German messages. Further
work after the war produced the Mark One, technically the first computer in the world, which was put into operation at Manchester
University in June 1948. Central to work on both machines was the
mathematician Alan Turing. Turing was brilliant, eccentric, naively
honest and openly gay. The authorities were willing to overlook his sex-
uality during the war, but in 1952 Turing was convicted of 'gross
indecency'. He was punished by a year of 'chemical castration'—he was
given female hormones, which rendered him impotent and caused him to
grow breasts. In 1954 Turing killed himself.[35]

The Mark One was built as the prototype of a machine which could be
mass produced by the Ferranti electronics company. But the British computer industry never competed effectively with its US rival. ENIAC,
forerunner of the first American computer, was completed in 1945; it had
been designed to calculate tables used in aiming artillery pieces, and was
later used to do calculations on the first hydrogen bombs. By the early
1950s various different computers were in operation.

It was at this point that IBM began to make computers. The company
had evolved from the Tabulating Machine Company, who sold calculating machines to the US Census Bureau. Now the Census Bureau
began buying computers from their competitors Remington Rand. The
more forward-looking IBM executives realised that the company was
doomed if it continued to ignore computers. However, Thomas Watson
Senior, who had run the company since 1914, was unconvinced and only
agreed to make computers when the US government asked IBM to do so
during the Korean War.[36] During the next 20 years much of the development of computers was funded by the US state, which needed ever

smaller and more powerful machines—to control missiles, for example, and to guide spacecraft as part of the Apollo programme.[37] The US government invested $400 million in IBM, for example, to ensure it kept ahead in the technological arms race.[38] The first 20 years of computing, then, does nothing to support the idea that the market works best without the intervention of the state. The second 20 years, in the 1970s and 1980s, demonstrates that the market, far from making the best in new technologies rapidly available, has brought chaos at every turn.

The fall of IBM and the rise of Microsoft

IBM was generally considered to be one of the most stable and profitable companies in the world when it announced that in 1992 it had made a $5 billion loss—the largest in commercial history. In the first half of 1993 alone IBM lost a further $8.3 billion.[39] The company finally returned to profitability in 1994—by the end of that year they had sacked some 35,000 people.[40] IBM's fall has been matched by the rise of software company Microsoft. First created in 1975, Microsoft has risen to dominate the computer software industry, making its founder and chief executive, Bill Gates, the richest man in the world. How did such a turnaround happen?

At the height of IBM's success more than 70 percent of the world's computer installations were based on its equipment. The company had invested $5 billion in the early 1960s on the development of a range of computers called the 360. The 360 range was technically advanced and different sizes of machines were available—a company could start off with a small machine and easily upgrade to a bigger one. Developing the 360 was a gamble, since the technology might not have worked, and the 360 made obsolete all previously available IBM computers. But the gamble paid off and IBM became enormously profitable.[41] By the 1980s, IBM's profits funded an immense bureaucracy. Writing in 1989, Chris Harman quoted the *Wall Street Journal* to the effect that IBM was:

> [a] *giant, calcified institution in desperate need of structural modernisation... Even after slashing its workforce the colossus is one of the world's most luxuriantly thick bureaucracies... IBM budget planners write reports about coming reports.*[42]

This was not an accident peculiar to IBM—Harman notes the same process taking place in the car industry, the direct result of the operation of the market. With consistent profit levels IBM had little need to innovate. The company became so large that different parts of it judged their work by purely internal criteria, regardless of how profitable it might be for the company as a whole. This became clear when IBM began to collaborate with Microsoft to write software. IBM measured how much work someone did by how much programming code they wrote. This sounds reasonable but the most efficient software uses as few programming instructions as possible for each task since this means it can run more quickly. In this case:

> ...a Microsoft developer took a piece of IBM code that required 33,000 characters of space and rewrote it in 200 characters... This was considered rude. Other Microsoft developers then rewrote other parts of IBM's code to make it faster and smaller. This was even ruder. IBM managers then began complaining that, according to their management system, Microsoft hadn't been pulling its weight. Measured in lines of code, they said, Microsoft was actually doing **negative** work...[43]

IBM's conservatism and bureaucracy finally caught up with it when they came to produce their personal computer (PC) in 1981. IBM had been trying for several years to produce a successful small computer. In the end they succeeded by assembling a group of mavericks from throughout the company and giving them only a year to put a machine together—an extremely short time by IBM's ponderous standards. The PC developers produced the computer on schedule by buying many of the machine's components from outside suppliers, rather than producing them within IBM. At first the PC was an enormous success—in the first four months of the PC's existence, sales reached $40 million.[44] But other manufacturers could buy the parts that made up a PC from the same suppliers as IBM and they did so, producing 'clones'—machines which worked just the same way as an IBM PC but cost less. For a while, both IBM and the clone manufacturers made impressive profits, which further reinforced IBM's complacent belief that it would always dominate the computer industry.

After 1985 such complacency led to disaster. IBM, which made millions from leasing large computers to large companies, never considered that selling small computers might one day be the more important market. It was used to the longer development times which had worked with the big old mainframe computers, and so it didn't update its PC as technology developed. Instead IBM tried to change the technology which the clone manufacturers were copying—they introduced a new computer called the PS/2 which worked differently, and stopped selling the PC which had been so popular. In this way it hoped to drive out the clones and completely control the market. But the new computer performed no better than the old ones. As one former IBM executive commented about his managers, 'They still didn't realise they were in a competitive world. They thought we could ram anything down customers' throats.' Meanwhile, clone manufacturers quickly improved their machines as new technology came along. When IBM's new computer failed, it was forced to return to making PCs. But now, as one account of IBM's decline puts it, 'IBM was just another clone maker, but the one with the most pretensions, the biggest overhead, the highest prices, and a rapidly falling market share.'[45] IBM's share of the now enormous personal computer market fell from 50 percent in 1984 to 8 percent in 1995, and its profits fell with it.[46]

In retrospect, IBM seems foolish not to have recognised the importance of personal computers. But there are many new technologies which fail in the marketplace, from 8 track tape cartridges to electric cars, and there is no way of knowing which will become important. Technical superiority is no guarantee of success—Betamax was a technically better video system than VHS, and BSB's satellite broadcasting system better than Sky's. The only way of finding out which will work is to gamble—as IBM did successfully with the 360 and the PC, and unsuccessfully with the PS/2. In the circumstances it seems unsurprising that IBM tended to stick with products with a proven record of profitability rather than innovating. The market gave it no incentive to do so.

As IBM's fortunes have declined, so those of Microsoft and Bill Gates have risen. This may look like a capitalist dream come true—that anyone with brains and who works hard can become rich—but the reality is rather different. Gates first got involved with computers at 13 years of age. The son of upper middle class parents, he attended a school rich enough to pay for the students to have use of a computer, which was exceptional in 1968. Gates then dropped out of university to work with computers with schoolmate Paul Allen. One popular history gives the following account:

> Like the Buddha, Gates's enlightenment came in a flash. Walking across Harvard Yard while Paul Allen waved in his face the January 1975 issue of **Popular Electronics** announcing the Altair 8800 microcomputer from MITS, they both saw instantly that there would really be a personal computer industry and that the industry would need programming languages. Although there were no microcomputer software companies yet, 19 year old Bill's first concern was that they were already too late. 'We realised that the revolution might happen without us,' Gates said. 'After we saw that article, there was no question of where our life would focus.'[47]

We are to believe that Gates became rich by single mindedly devoting his life to computer software after one insight of genius. The reality is more complex and grubbier.

Microsoft's success has been based for the last 15 years on software called MS-DOS, which was included with the IBM PC, and with all the clones made since. MS-DOS is an 'operating system', software which enables the different parts of a computer like the screen and keyboard to work together. IBM had originally hoped to buy an operating system from Microsoft's then competitors Digital Research. But the head of Digital Research, Gary Kildall, didn't even meet with IBM since he knew that all the small computers they had produced up to that point had failed, and he didn't see why the PC should be any different. His wife and business partner Dorothy was a lawyer and she was horrified by the legal constraints IBM wanted to place on Digital Research as part of the deal. So IBM went to Microsoft, and asked if they could buy an operating system from them instead. Microsoft agreed to sell an operating system to IBM—though they didn't actually have one to sell. Instead, they arranged with a neighbouring company to use one called QDOS, which they renamed MS-DOS and eventually bought outright. QDOS was all but copied from a third operating system, called CP/M and written by none other than Gary Kildall of Digital Research. The success of MS-DOS starts with a lucky break and a dodgy business deal, not with intelligence and hard work.[48]

As the story of MS-DOS went on, Gates continued to be lucky. IBM and each clone manufacturer paid Microsoft a fee for each computer they sold with MS-DOS, so the enormous sales of PCs and clones meant big profits. IBM, of course, was unhappy to pay Microsoft so much money for a product Microsoft was also selling to IBM's competitors. They wanted to get control of the operating system back and so kill off the clones. With the PS/2, IBM introduced a new operating system, OS/2. Microsoft could only sell an inferior version of OS/2 to clone manufacturers. The full version was to be sold only by IBM and only worked on IBM computers.[49] But, when the PS/2 flopped, OS/2 flopped with it, and Microsoft went on profitably selling MS-DOS to clone manufacturers.

Gates's success was based on his initial judgement that PCs would be immensely successful, and on his undoubted abilities and hard work. But it was also based on an entirely unlikely set of circumstances—that IBM would license an operating system from Microsoft for the PC, would make a success of the PC, and then hand that market over to their competitors. After all, if the PC hadn't sold, neither would have MS-DOS. If the PS/2 had sold, MS-DOS would have become redundant. Rather than being based on Gates's abilities—or the high quality of MS-DOS— Microsoft's success in the 1980s was due to a series of lucky breaks. All this is very far from the theory of a self regulating market delivering the best goods at the lowest price.

The market and the mouse

The second piece of software which has been central to Microsoft's profitability is Windows. Windows made computers easier to use. Earlier computer screens had been black with white characters—with Windows the screen was white with black writing, like paper. Rather than typing in commands, you moved a pointer about the screen with a device called a 'mouse'. You used the mouse to choose what you wanted to do from lists called 'menus', which appeared and vanished as you needed and finished with them, or you chose from little pictures called 'icons'. Windows has been one of the most successful pieces of software ever sold. You might imagine that, when it came to market in 1990, Microsoft had just invented it. Yet the mouse was invented in the 1960s, and everything else that was distinctive about Windows had existed since 1973.[50]

In the early 1970s there had been much discussion about computers creating a 'paperless office'—documents would be created on computers, be edited and stored on computers, and sent to a person's computer for them to read. At no point would the document exist on paper. This idea worried Xerox, whose business was photocopiers, and which was aware that its patents on the photocopying process would some day expire. It set up a research establishment called PARC to explore computers. By 1973, PARC had produced the Alto. The Alto had a black on white screen, had icons and menus, and had a mouse. Altos could be linked together using a technology called Ethernet, still used today, and printed documents using the world's first laser printers— again, a technology still used today. In fact the Alto included all the technologies to be marketed so successfully by Microsoft 17 years later. However, Xerox took so little interest in the Alto that it didn't even patent the technologies involved. It worked out that such a machine wouldn't be profitable to produce, and then forgot it.[51]

In December 1979 Xerox bought $1 million worth of shares in a new computer company called Apple. As part of the deal a group from Apple were given a tour of PARC. Apple boss Steve Jobs was amazed that Xerox wasn't exploiting the technology it had developed: "'Why aren't you doing anything with this?" he bellowed. "This is the greatest thing! This is revolutionary!'"[52]

Apple decided to produce a machine which worked in a similar way to the Alto, called the Macintosh. After years of development (the project was cancelled on several occasions) the Macintosh came on the market in 1984. Early sales were disappointing, but in 1985 new software and an Apple version of the 'laser printer' pioneered by Xerox PARC became available. These made the Macintosh capable of doing 'desktop publishing'—people with no specialist training could use their computers to do typesetting and graphic design. The Macintosh established a niche in the market which it has hung on to ever since.[53]

Apple had approached Microsoft in 1981 to produce software for the Macintosh. After they began working with Apple, Microsoft produced Windows, their own version of the Alto's system. Bill Gates wanted, in the words of one Microsoft manager, a 'Mac on a PC'—in fact, Windows resembled Macintosh software to such an extent that Apple sued Microsoft for breach of copyright in 1988, finally losing the case in 1992. Perhaps the most accurate summary of the relationship between Windows, the Macintosh and the Alto is a comment Bill Gates made to Steve Jobs in 1983: 'It's…like we both have this rich neighbour named Xerox, and you broke in to steal the TV set, and you found out that I'd been there first and you said, "Hey, that's not fair! I wanted to steal the TV set!"'[54] Far from bringing new technology promptly to market, Microsoft made enormous profits from technology which was 17 years old, much of which had been developed by other companies.

From fighting the system to fighting for market share

The fall of IBM and the rise of companies like Microsoft and Apple is not a new phenomenon, but typical of the workings of capitalism. Marx and Engels wrote in the *Communist Manifesto,* 'Constant revolutionising of production, uninterrupted disturbance of all social conditions, ever-lasting uncertainty and agitation distinguish the bourgeois epoch from all earlier ones.'[55] Companies and whole industries grow and decline as part of the search for profit. However, personal computers began to develop in the wake of the radicalisation of the 1960s. The first such machines were developed by people who built them as a hobby, who met together and shared ideas freely. For people from this milieu it was easy to confuse fighting IBM politically by challenging capitalism as a system, with fighting IBM in the marketplace. The confusion was all the easier to make because the styles of the old and new companies were very different. IBM executives all wore the same blue suits. Microsoft employees slept under their desks when a project needed finishing. One coped with the exhaustion by learning to sleep standing up.[56] Designers of part of the Macintosh at one point 'were staying up 58 hours straight, blasting Dead Kennedys records, gobbing Vitamin C like popcorn.' One played video games to relax, while another 'would just sit there and scream, top of his lungs'.

Apple founder Steve Jobs encouraged his staff to believe that this kind of thing showed that they were rebelling against the system:

> *One of Jobs's slogans proclaimed, 'IT'S BETTER TO BE A PIRATE THAN JOIN THE NAVY.' Forget that they were employees of a billion dollar corpo-*

ration—the Mac team was a raucous band of buccaneers, answering to no one but their Captain!

As the 1960s faded their legacy was seen not in terms of collective struggle, but of individual fulfillment and self expression. This fitted with the idea that the new companies were successful because they recruited such clever, if eccentric, people. Certainly it is true that employment at Microsoft or Apple has been very different from most work under capitalism—the exceptional profitability of the companies meant that class struggle hardly existed. Many Microsoft employees, paid partly in company shares, became millionaires as the company grew. Extraordinary levels of identification with the employer were the norm—one ex-Apple manager remembered, 'For a month after I left, I cried myself to sleep.' This state of things was reinforced by the fact that many workers were hired straight from college—with no experience of work or domestic commitments, they were happy to work insanely hard for the chance to make big money—and if it got too much, they could sell their shares at 30 and leave.

For some workers, the new computer firms had been part of an idealistic, reformist project—to give people more power against large companies by making available small, cheap, powerful computers. In the words of an Apple staff member:

Very few of us were even thirty years old... We all felt as though we had missed the civil rights movement. We had missed Vietnam. What we had was the Macintosh.[57]

Amid the glamour of high profits the ideal of changing the world became that of making a cosy niche in the world, with computers as tools for self expression—the ultimate aim of life of the new middle class of managers and professionals which many ex-students had by now joined.

The development of the internet

Far from marking the end of industrial capitalism and the state, the internet has always depended on them. In 1957 the Soviet Union launched Sputnik, the first artificial satellite. There was considerable alarm among the US ruling class who needed to constantly better Soviet technology so as to keep ahead in the arms race. The US government set up ARPA, an agency with the job of ensuring the US military had the most advanced technology possible. One problem which ARPA considered was that of maintaining communications systems in the event of nuclear war. They worried that the destruction of only a small number of cities could bring all communications to a standstill because the systems weren't sufficiently flexible. If the phone lines from, for example, New York to Washington were blown up there was no way those cities could communicate. If New York were destroyed, all the communications systems centred in New York would be useless. In 1969 ARPA created a computer network, ARPANET, which addressed these problems. Messages were sent around the network by computers, which constantly informed each other about the state of the network. If one part of the network vanished, the computers told each other this, and messages were sent by routes which remained undamaged.[58]

ARPANET, used by military and academic institutions, grew to connect 562 computer systems in 1983, in which year the military left to set up their own network. The following year, the US National Science Foundation took over running the system, now known as the internet, and they did this until the system was privatised in 1994—by this time over 2 million computer systems were connected.[59] As with all other areas of computing, then, the internet received massive initial funding from the state, particularly the military. The market was in no way involved—indeed, for most of the internet's history commercial activity has been banned from the system.

Computers today—the market

The history of computers does nothing to support the idea that the free market delivers choice or efficiency. In fact, far from having developed beyond a Marxist analysis, computers show many of the features by which Marxists have characterised capitalism. Since Marx's own time, capitalist economies have been prone to booms and slumps. The profitability of a particular area of the economy encourages capitalists to invest in it in ever greater numbers. After a certain point more of the commodities involved are being produced than can be sold. The price of the commodity falls, driving down profits and putting the weaker capitalists out of business. This leads to a shortage of the commodity, so that prices begin to rise and the whole cycle can start again. The making of semiconductors, the chips which control computers as well as CD players and many other electrical appliances, has followed just this pattern. In 1995 the world market for semiconductors was growing by over 30 percent a year. Net profits were as high as 50 percent. As a result around 50 semiconductor factories were planned around the world, each costing around $1 billion. However, in August 1995 the *Financial Times* reported that institutional investors were wary when Korean electronics company Tatung planned to build such a plant: 'The risk is that the planned semiconductor venture is mistimed and comes on-line when the industry, notorious for its punishing boom-and-bust profit cycles, has entered a downtrend.'

Indeed by 1996 more chips were produced than the market would bear, and prices fell—one chip which was selling at $46 at the start of the year cost only $11 by September. Investment decreased and new plants were put on hold as profits declined.[60]

Defenders of capitalism argue that the market leads to innovation and choice. But in fact the economy is increasingly dominated by a small number of firms. For example, the aerospace industry is dominated by three companies—Boeing, McDonnell Douglas and Lockheed. And, as this article was being written, the first two of these announced a merger. A few supermarket chains sell most of the groceries bought in Britain. Computers are no different. As we have seen already, the industry of the 1960s was completely dominated by IBM. In 1995 six companies made 46 percent of the personal computers sold, and their domination of the market was expected to increase in 1996, perhaps reaching 75 percent by the end of the decade. Most of these computers use chips made by Intel, which has an 80 percent share of the world market.[61] Much of the software for these machines is made by Microsoft, which completely dominates the market for operating systems with MS-DOS and Windows. Microsoft also supplies a majority of personal computer business software—databases, spreadsheets and word processing. Their nearest rival is Lotus, which recently became a subsidiary of IBM. Even markets which have only developed recently are dominated by one company. To use the world wide web system on the internet, you need software called a 'browser'. Some 74 percent of use of the web takes place through the most popular browser, Netscape—the nearest competitor accounts for only 8 percent of use.[62]

Relations between the large companies which dominate the computer industry are far from the straightforward competition which market enthusiasts might expect. We have already seen the shifting pattern of co-operation and competition which existed in the 1980s between IBM, Microsoft and Apple. In 1995 Toshiba and IBM were planning to build a joint semiconductor plant in the US, while Toshiba, IBM and Siemens were collaborating on chip development in Germany, where Philips and IBM were also developing a joint plant. Japanese chip manufacturers were considering working together on some projects to stay ahead of foreign competition.[63] This network of partial co-operation is matched by a complex pattern of ownership between leading computer companies. Motorola, France Telecom and NEC, for example, each own 17 percent of Groupe Bull. NEC and Groupe Bull each own 19.99 percent of Packard Bell.[64] In 1995, ICL—84 percent owned by Fujitsu—bought a controlling stake in Germany's fifth largest computer manufacturer, while Amstrad bought Jarfalla, a Swedish company once owned by

IBM.[65] All of these temporary alliances, and this jockeying for position, are entirely unlike the 'rigour of competition' which is supposed to characterise the market.

Billions have been spent on information technology on the assumption that it increases productivity. But there is remarkably little evidence that it actually gives value for money. A 1995 survey of financial insitutions, for example, found that only 28 percent felt that information technology delivered the financial return required of it, 34 percent didn't know, while 38 percent felt that it didn't deliver financially. US economists Stephen Oliver and Daniel Sichel have claimed that between 1970 and 1992, computers have only added 0.3 percent to the growth in economic output.[66] It seems remarkable that capitalists invest huge sums in technology which might actually be losing them money, but the market makes it inevitable. In March 1995, for example, Chase Manhattan Bank spent some $100 million on a new computerised trading floor. It was unlikely that the new technology would generate enough profit to pay for itself, the *Financial Times* reported, but the investment was necessary so that Chase Manhattan could compete with other banks, who were spending even more on information technology.[67] A similar logic lies behind much of the hype about the internet. An advert for Apple's world wide web software puts it in these terms:

> *Let's face it, the expansion of the internet is a phenomenon to be ignored at your peril. Thousands of companies are already on the world wide web, from fledgling start-ups to large international corporations—and the chances are, your competitors are already there.*
>
> *The question is, if you're not on the web today, where will your business be tomorrow?*[68]

We have already seen that only a small number of people have access to the internet. For some companies, the costs of being 'on the web' will exceed the profits generated. None the less, those companies have to join the stampede for fear that their competitors will steal business from them. Market competition actually lowers levels of profitability.

In fact the logic of the market generates huge problems for the computer industry. One such problem is that posed by the year 2000. Much of the software governments and businesses currently use assumes that all years start with '19' and only the last two numbers ever change. No one knows how such software will behave after the end of 1999. Changing all the systems involved is potentially a huge and expensive task—16 percent of companies say it will cost them between £2 and £5 million, and 15 percent say it will cost over £5 million. However, many companies are ignoring the whole issue. Almost half have no strategy for dealing with the problem. Asked when their systems will be able to cope with the year 2000, 21 percent of companies say only in 1999 or 2000, while 5 percent say after the year 2000. Given the fact that information technology projects seldom meet deadlines, it is possible that many computer systems will grind to a halt after the end of 1999. According to the business publication *Computer Weekly*:

> *The current state of debate about the year 2000 is chillingly reminiscent of the last hours of the **Titanic**. The industry is split between those who are crying doom and disaster and those who are pooh poohing all the fuss as being wildly out of control.*

The market makes it impossible to assess how severe the problem actually is. On the one hand, analysts and consultants are keen to stress the potential problems so as to get companies to pay them for sorting those problems out. On the other hand, managers dread taking on a project which will be a disaster if it doesn't deliver on time and which will cost a lot of money with no prospect of a return. 'The dilemma facing information technology managers is to steer a sensible path between the get-rich-quick doomwatch merchants who would obviously like to hussle everybody onto their books, and the head-in-the-sand ostriches oblivious of the tidal wave approaching.'[69]

The market also ensures that vast sums of money are wasted on failed computer projects. Gloucestershire Social Services spent between £300,000 and £1 million on a computer system which came into operation in 1993. It was so slow and complicated to use that in January 1995 they were planning to spend up to £200,000 on a new one. *Computer Weekly* explains that computer companies have to promise the moon so as to win contracts:

> *The problem for suppliers in general is that if they pointed out all the risks associated with major projects...they would lose the business... Consequently suppliers promise everything during the bidding process in the sincere hope that they will be able to deliver...*[70]

The state

In addition to the claims of the free market enthusiasts that the state has no useful economic role to play, the 1990s have seen the growth of theories of 'globalisation'. According to these, international trade has grown to a level where multinational companies can move production from country to country as they see fit. As a result, if governments impose high taxes on profits, or workers receive high wages, the companies involved will simply move to countries which don't reduce their profits in this way. The state is powerless before the market.[71]

Computers would seem to be one of the industries most likely to be affected by globalisation. Thousands of chips are so small that they can be loaded on a plane and flown round the world at little cost—surely companies can manufacture them wherever they like? With wages for software engineers in India less than a quarter of those in Germany, why shouldn't software companies do all their development in poorer countries and save money? Yet this isn't what happens. As far as the location of a semiconductor plant is concerned, the *Financial Times* explains:

> *Basic requirements include an adequate labour force, reliable utilities, clean air and copious water supplies. Chipmakers also look for sites that are well-served by the suppliers of the chemicals and equipment used in semiconductor production…semiconductor manufacturers are not lured by low cost labour. Typically, labour accounts for less than 10 percent of the cost of running a semiconductor factory—with depreciation of the plant being a much bigger factor.*

According to one manager from leading chipmaker Intel:

> *The politics and other financial inducements are much more important than the salary structure. If you get tax relief…or training grants or capital equipment grants, those are much more important than salaries.*[72]

For example, in August 1995 Siemens announced that it would invest over $1 billion in a chip plant on Tyneside. Siemens chose to locate the plant in the UK against competition from Ireland and Austria, it was reported, after 'intensive lobbying by Mr Michael Heseltine…and the personal intervention of Mr John Major'. All three governments had offered Siemens incentives packages—the UK government package was worth 'close to £50 million'. According to Siemens, its reasons for choosing the UK included 'the availability of a flexible labour force, good infrastructure and a proven track record in the industry and a sizeable domestic market for semiconductors…'[73]

Factors such as reliable infrastructure, experience in semiconductor production and a large domestic market are available in relatively few countries. For this reason, the United States has 33 percent of the world semiconductor market, followed by Japan with 29 percent, and then by South Korea, Germany and the UK.[74] Manufacturers do plan to expand into other countries—in the autumn of 1995, for example, there were seven chip manufacturing plants being planned in China.[75] But this is not because of lower wages, but because of the growth of the domestic market in a country where 700,000 personal computers were sold in 1994 and the market expands by some 30 percent a year. Compaq, the largest personal computer manufacturer in the world, follows a similar rationale—it has plants in Texas, Scotland and Singapore, and is planning new ones in China and Brazil 'in preparation for the expected rapid growth of PCs in developing markets'.[76]

Manufacturers thus still depend on states to provide infrastructure such as transport and electricity supplies, and financial incentives to pay for new plants. Governments like the British Tories, acting in complete opposition to their free market rhetoric, use the state to sponsor industry. The state thus continues to be as central to capitalism as it always was and, as far as software goes, its role in policing copyright and patents is essential. Copying computer software is usually easy to do, and the copy is of exactly the same quality as the original. Illegal copying is estimated to cost the computer industry some £400 million a year. The UK software industry, for example, is demanding that British and European parliaments act to strengthen copyright law. The US government has threatened sanctions against China if action is not taken to reduce software piracy—it is estimated that some 94 percent of software in China is pirated, and the US company Microsoft is badly affected.[77]

The discrepancy between the rhetoric and the reality of capitalism concerning the state means that defenders of the system often end up contradicting themselves. Bill Gates, for example, reports with enthusiasm that in Singapore the state is forcing builders to construct a computer infrastructure:

Every developer will soon be required to provide every new house or apartment with a broadband cable in the same way he is required by law to provide lines for water, gas, electricity and telephone. When I visited with Lee Kuan Yew, the 72 year old senior minister who was the political head of Singapore from 1959 to 1990, I was extremely impressed with his understanding of the opportunity...

But only three pages later, Gates is concerned that state intervention will be a bureaucratic drag on market efficiency:

In many countries nowadays, top political leaders are making plans to encourage highway investment [ie information superhighway, or computer communications, investment—CW]... A government bootstrap could, in principle, cause an information highway to be built sooner than might happen otherwise, but the very real possibility of an unattractive outcome has to be considered carefully. Such a country might end up with a boondoggle, white-elephant information highway built by engineers out of touch with the rapid pace of technological development.[78]

Scott McNealy of Sun Microsystems gave the *Financial Times* an even more confused account of how capitalism works:

Microsoft is getting into all sorts of businesses...its dominant position is unhealthy for the market, says Mr McNealy... It is stunning how few people understand market economics... There is a huge amount of ignorance... We have great empirical evidence that choice works, and that is why we have anti-trust and consent decrees to control the market.[79]

The free market works fine by itself, apparently, as long as the state regularly intervenes in it.

Computers and the working class

Computers have made an enormous difference to the jobs of many workers in the developed countries. Information technology spending per employee is highest in white collar jobs such as banking and finance (£6,243 per year) and insurance (£5,505), followed by central government (£4,324) and local government (£3,310)—though in engineering the figure is still high (£1,598).[80] Many would claim that the development of computers has reduced the numbers of jobs available, and reduced the power of those still in work to defend their jobs and conditions.

The workers who use computers today have not traditionally been seen as part of the working class. Fifty years ago bank workers, civil servants and local government white collar staff were thought to be in a relatively privileged position. Such white collar employment meant a 'job for life' on good pay. If such workers did join unions, they were often more like staff associations which had a cosy relationship with management and never went on strike. All this has changed. White collar work has been routinised, job security has vanished, pay has fallen, and unions such as UNISON, CPSA and BIFU have all been involved in strike action. However different their conditions of work, or their traditions, from such traditional working class figures as miners, dockers or shipbuilders, such workers have found they can only defend themselves by uniting through their unions to oppose management attacks. The fact that white collar workers form an increasingly large part of the working class, therefore, does not mean workers have less power.

In some industries, such as printing national newspapers, the introduction of computers has coincided with job losses. But job losses in the print were more the result of union leaders' failure to stand up to employers' attacks than a direct consequence of computerisation in itself. Other areas, such as local government, have introduced computers without large staff cuts. And if advances in technology have destroyed some jobs, they have created others—in 1995, for example, chip manufacturer Motorola became the largest industrial employer in Scotland.[81]

Some people worry that computers will make possible a society like that depicted in George Orwell's *Nineteen Eighty-Four*, where the state is able to spy on every aspect of peoples' lives and so make it impossible to fight back. For example, they argue that virtually all purchases will soon be made using computerised barcode systems and credit or debit cards, so that computers will constantly gather information about where people are, the kind of things they buy, and so on. Of course, people are right to be concerned that information held about them on computers should be accurate, private and so forth. But the nightmare of a computerised police state isn't likely to happen. We have already seen that, far from being efficient and all knowing, computers are as badly made as any other commodity produced under capitalism. As for the state, the Department of Social Security spent £2.6 billion between 1984 and 1996 on a computer system designed to administer welfare benefits—in theory cutting costs and making it possible to cut over 20,000 staff. In fact, by 1996 staff numbers had risen by 2,000, and the computer system needed a further £750 million spent on it before it would work properly.[82] Meanwhile the Department of Health has been setting up computer systems to keep records on every person in the UK. But the DSS and DoH never discussed co-ordinating their computer projects, though such co-ordination would have saved hundreds of millions of pounds.[83] If the government can't even use computers effectively to pay benefits or keep track of medical records, there is little chance that they could use them to constantly spy on everybody. Anyone who successfully avoided paying the poll tax, or who has received the wrong amount of benefit or none at all 'because of a problem with the computer', has a much better idea of the level of information technology available to the national and local state.

Nor is it true that workers in high technology companies have little power. We have seen that such companies can't simply relocate to low wage countries if workers in the developed world fight for better pay or conditions. In the first place, such countries lack the necessary infrastructure. In the second, a company with a substantial investment in machinery—at the most, as we have seen, a chip plant costing $1 billion—can't simply pick it up and move it elsewhere. Indeed, the size of such investments, and their rapid depreciation, means workers in such plants have immense power. The speed of technological development means that chip factories rapidly become obsolete. In the words of Intel management, 'If you make $2 billion dollars capital investment, the bulk of capital investment is written off in four years, and on $2 billion that is $500 million a year depreciation.'[84] Such a plant therefore has to make over $9 million a week simply to pay for its construction costs. If workers strike for even a short time they cause the company massive losses.

Other computer workers have similar potential power. In February 1995 Norwich Union sacked 93 information technology staff. The staff were called to a meeting where they were given their redundancy notices. Their identity cards were taken from them, they were then accompanied to their desks by security staff while they packed, and they were then escorted from the building. They were given no time to say goodbye to other workers, or to make any phone calls. *Computer Weekly* explained:

> *This brutal procedure is becoming the standard way for companies to dispose of anyone with a sensitive job. The idea is to protect the business from sabotage by supervising employees' speedy exit, preventing them from tampering with computers in a fit of revenge.*[85]

These extreme precautions meant Norwich Union workers didn't get a chance to use their power, but in March 1996 a group of civil servants did. *Computer Weekly* reported that:

> *Strike action by just eleven Courts Service computer staff will lead to £4 million in uncollected debts and 100,000 unissued summonses a month until the dispute is resolved.*

> *Staff at the Courts Agency Computer Centre in Northampton began a two week strike on Monday. They are protesting over being forced to transfer out of the civil service to a private contractor...*[86]

Computer workers have the ability to cause widespread disruption in official and financial systems—at a time when increased unionisation and management attacks make it likely that times will come when they use that power.

How should socialists respond to information technology?

The claim that we live in a post-industrial information society, in which the free market delivers and Marxism is outdated, is false. Rather, the development of computers *strengthens* the Marxist case. For Marx, the development of the means of production was the bedrock on which social change rested:

At a certain stage of development, the material productive forces of society come into conflict with the existing relations of production or—this merely expresses the same thing in legal terms—with the property relations within the framework of which they have operated hitherto. From forms of development of the productive forces those relations turn into their fetters. Then begins an era of social revolution. The changes in the economic foundation lead sooner or later to the transformation of the whole immense superstructure.[87]

The transition from feudalism to capitalism, and the revolutionary upheavals it involved, occurred when social structures such as the medieval church and absolute monarchy came to prevent the development of the forces of production. They were replaced by social forms such as bourgeois democracy, wage labour and formal equality before the law, which made possible the development of productive forces to a level undreamt of under feudalism. But those social forms, progressive in their day, in turn become outmoded as the forces of production advance. The overthrow of capitalism now becomes necessary for humanity's productive potential to be realised.

For example, there is today no technical reason why in each village and town on earth there should not exist a link to a worldwide computer network. From the network anyone would be able to obtain, in a few minutes, a copy of any book ever published, any piece of music ever recorded, any film or TV programme ever made. The educational and cultural opportunties which such a system would bring to billions of people are beyond imagining. Yet such a system could only be built in a socialist society. You see why when you consider Bill Gates's account of how people could use a computer network ('the highway') to do this kind of thing under capitalism:

Record companies, or even individual recording artists, might choose to sell music in a new way. You, the consumer, won't need compact discs, tapes, or any other kinds of physical apparatus. The music will be stored as bits of information on a server [a large computer—CW] *on the highway. 'Buying' a song or album will really mean buying the right to access the appropriate bits...in any non-commercial setting, anywhere you go, you'll have the right to play the song without additional payment to the copyright holder. In the same way, the information highway could keep track of whether you had bought the right to read a particular book or see a movie.*

Computers that could be used to make the world's culture universally available are to be used to exclude those who have not paid the fee. The system can only exist if it includes an immense sub-system for checking who has bought what—the computerised equivalent of keeping tabs on the record collection of everyone in the world. Concepts like private property and copyright, which once helped the development of production, have now become a hindrance to it. If you compare Gates's vision of the future with the political and cultural achievements of capitalism in earlier periods, what is most remarkable is its staggering banality. For example:

> *If you are watching the movie **Top Gun** and think Tom Cruise's aviator sunglasses look really cool, you'll be able to pause the movie and learn about the glasses or even buy them on the spot... If the movie's star carries a handsome leather briefcase or handbag, the highway will let you browse the manufacturer's entire line of leather goods and either order one or be directed to a convenient retailer.*

The queries Gates thinks we might want to put to such a computer system include, 'List all the stores that carry two or more kinds of dog food and will deliver a case within 60 minutes to my home address,' and 'Which major city has the greatest percentage of the people who watch rock videos and regularly read about international trade?'[88]

Such poverty of ideas is not so much the result of Gates's personality as of the logic of capitalism. By the autumn of 1996, for example, four British supermarket chains had issued a total of 19 million loyalty cards. For each card issued, computers collect information about every tin of beans and box of teabags that customers purchase. British Gas, which is currently claiming that if it is forced to reduce prices it will have to lay off staff, has spent £150 million on a new billing system. The government has spent £70 million on a new jobcentre computer system, as part of cutting benefits to the unemployed.[89] Again, routine administrative tasks are ideally suited to computerisation—but it is just as computers come to be widespread that we also see a huge expansion in routine clerical work. At Computer Associates, the third largest software company in the world, management have turned off the electronic mail—the computer communications system—for much of the day because staff were responding too eagerly to it. The marketing director commented that 'the e-mail would come in and they would drop everything to deal with it', and explained to clients that 'if it mattered that much, you'd have phoned'.[90] Time and again, technology which could improve people's lives is used in a way which is either pointless or actually makes those lives worse.

Now, as in Marx's time, capitalism is capable of enormous technical advances—the benefits of which it denies to all but a few. But information technology also makes clear how capitalism has outlived its ability to take human society forward. Instead, as computers and the internet develop, they give a new resonance to Marx and Engels' claim that:

[after] *the overthrow of the existing state of society by the communist revolution... the liberation of each single individual will be accomplished in the measure in which history becomes transformed into world history...it is clear that the real intellectual wealth of the individual depends entirely on the wealth of his real connections. Only then will the separate individuals be liberated from the various national and local barriers, be brought into practical connection with the material and intellectual production of the whole world and be put in a position to acquire the capacity to enjoy this all-sided production of the whole earth...*[91]

Notes

References in italics starting *ftp*, *gopher* or *http* identify documents on the internet. In agreement with *International Socialism* I have used references in the notes below which are only available on the internet since so much information about the net is only available on the net itself. Internet references, however, are not generally acceptable in *International Socialism* articles. Unlike books, there is as yet no guarantee that the original reference will still be available in five or ten years time. And, without wishing to overstate the editorial or scholarly control exercised over the publication of some books, internet articles often do not go through even the minimum of preparation common in many publishing houses.

1   *The Guardian*, 2 May 1996.
2   B Gates, *The Road Ahead* (London, 1995), pp74-6.
3   Microsoft/Intelliquest National Computing Survey, pp58-59. Available from *http://www.microsoft.com*
4   Back cover of D Spender, *Nattering on the Net: Women, Power and Cyberspace* (North Melbourne, 1995).
5   *Computer Weekly*, 18 April 1996.
6   Introduction, *Communicating Britain's Future*, *http://www.poptel.org.uk/labour-party/policy/info-highway/index.html*
7   B Gates, op cit, p183.
8   *Computer Weekly*, 12 January 1995.
9   *Marxism Today*, October 1988.
10 For the economy, see C Harman, 'The Myth of Market Socialism,' *International Socialism* 42, 'The State and Capitalism Today,' *International Socialism* 51 and 'Where is Capitalism Going?' *International Socialism* 58 and 60. A Callinicos, *Against Postmodernism: a Marxist Critique* (Cambridge, 1989) addresses many of the philosophical questions raised by computer and particularly internet enthusiasts.
11 J Palfreman and D Swade, *The Dream Machine: Exploring the Computer Age* (BBC Books, 1991), p8.
12 *Financial Times*, 2 May 1995.
13 *Financial Times*, 3 August 1995.
14 *http://www.nw.com/zone/host-count-history*
15 'Ensuring Social Use', *Communicating Britain's Future*, op cit.
16 Phones data from CIA World Factbook 1994, *gopher://UMSLVMA.UMSL.EDU:70/11/LIBRARY/GOVDOCS/WF93/WFLATEST*. Internet hosts from 'Host Distribution by Top-Level Domain Name,' January 1996, *http://www.nw.com/zone/WWW/dist-bynum.html*
17 E J Hobsbawm, *The Age of Empire 1875-1914* (London, 1989), p346.
18 'Microsoft/Intelliquest National Computing Survey,' op cit, p120.

19 O'Reilly and Associates, 'Defining the Internet Opportunity', *http://www.ora.com/survey/users/charts/pop-proj.html* and *http://www.ora.com/survey/users/charts/net-income.html*

20 'The Commercenet/Nielsen Internet Demographics Survey'—see *http://www.commerce.net/*

21 'Microsoft/Intelliquest National Computing Survey,' op cit, p10.

22 'The Graphic, Visualization and Usability Center's Fourth WWW User Survey', Georgia Institute of Technology, *http://www.gatech.edu*

23 'Microsoft/Intelliquest National Computing Survey,' op cit, pp11-12

24 B Gates, keynote speech, Interactive Media Conference, 6 June 1995—available from *http://www.microsoft.com*

25 'Ensuring Social Use', *Communicating Britain's Future*, op cit.

26 A Hyman, *Charles Babbage: Pioneer of the Computer* (Oxford, 1982), pp43-44.

27 D Swade, *Charles Babbage and his Calculating Engines* (London, 1991), p2.

28 A Hyman, op cit, pp52-53.

29 Ibid, pp169-170; D Swade, op cit, p10.

30 A Hyman, op cit, p198.

31 Ibid, pp90-92.

32 K Marx and F Engels, *Communist Manifesto*, see the edition printed in Beijing (1965), p39.

33 A Kidd, *Manchester* (Keele, 1993), pp116, 154.

34 E J Hobsbawm, *The Age of Revolution 1789-1848* (London, 1973), p216. See also C Harman, 'The State and Capitalism Today,' *International Socialism* 51, p11.

35 A Hodges, *Alan Turing, The Enigma of Intelligence* (London, 1985), ch 8.

36 J Palfreman and D Swade, op cit, chs 2 and 3.

37 Ibid, p91.

38 *The Observer*, 25 August 1996.

39 C H Ferguson and C R Morris, *Computer Wars: The Fall of IBM and the Future of Global Technology* (New York, 1994), pxi.

40 *Financial Times*, 12 January 1995.

41 C H Ferguson and C R Morris, op cit, ch 1.

42 'The Myth of Market Socialism', *International Socialism* 42, pp19-20.

43 P Carroll, *Big Blues: The Unmaking of IBM* (London, 1994), p101.

44 C H Ferguson and C R Morris, op cit, p28.

45 Ibid, p59.

46 *Computer Weekly*, 28 March 1996.

47 R X Cringely, *Accidental Empires* (London, 1993), p52.

48 S Manes and P Andrews, *Gates* (New York, 1994), chs 11 and 12.

49 Ibid, p331.

50 J Palfreman and D Swade, op cit, p99, which includes a photo of an early mouse.

51 S Manes and P Andrews, op cit, pp165-166; R X Cringely, op cit, pp82-83.

52 S Levy, *Insanely Great: The Life and Times of Macintosh, the Computer that Changed Everything* (London, 1995), p79.

53 Ibid, pp115, 186, 221.

54 S Manes and P Andrews, op cit, pp181-189, 225, 255, 357-364, 438.

55 K Marx and F Engels, op cit, p36.

56 S Manes and P Andrews, op cit, p211.

57 S Levy, op cit, pp143, 164, 175, 203.

58 H Reingold, *The Virtual Community: Finding Connection in a Computerised World*, (London, 1995), pp7, 71, 74.

59 B Sterling, *A Short History of the Internet, Internet Society* at *http://info.isoc.org:80/infosvc/index.html*; 'Number of Internet Hosts', *http://www.nw.com/zone/host-count-history*

60 *Financial Times*, 3 August 1995, 15 August 1995, 9 August 1995, 18 July 1995, 5 September 1995, 12 September 1996.
61 *Computer Weekly*, 28 March 1996, 4 January 1996; *Financial Times*, 5 April 1995.
62 *Computer Weekly*, 4 April 1996.
63 *Financial Times*, 9 August 1995, 27 September 1995, 11 July 1995.
64 *Financial Times*, 5 August 1995, 6 August 1995.
65 *Financial Times*, 30 March 1995, 14 June 1995.
66 *Computer Weekly*, 4 January 1996, 26 January 1995.
67 *Financial Times*, 31 March 1995.
68 *The Guardian*, 11 April 1996.
69 *Computer Weekly*, 4 April 1996, 18 April 1996, 21 March 1996.
70 *Computer Weekly*, 26 January 1995.
71 See C Harman, 'State and Capitalism Today', *International Socialism* 51, for a general refutation of these ideas.
72 *Financial Times*, 3 August 1995.
73 *Financial Times*, 5 August 1995.
74 *Financial Times*, 11 August 1995, 15 August 1995.
75 *Financial Times*, 27 September 1995.
76 *Financial Times*, 27 February 1995, 6 September 1995.
77 *Computer Weekly*, 4 January 1996, 9 February 1995.
78 B Gates, *The Road Ahead*, op cit, pp235, 238.
79 *Financial Times*, 3 May 1995.
80 *Computer Weekly*, 16 February 1995.
81 *Financial Times*, 1 July 1995.
82 *Computer Weekly*, 28 March 1996.
83 *Computer Weekly*, 30 March 1995.
84 *Financial Times*, 3 August 1995.
85 *Computer Weekly*, 9 February 1995.
86 *Computer Weekly*, 28 March 1996.
87 K Marx, 'Preface to A Contribution to the Critique of Political Economy', *Early Writings* (Harmondsworth, 1975), pp425-426.
88 B Gates, *The Road Ahead*, op cit, pp80, 165-166, 175-176.
89 *The Guardian*, 28 September 1996.
90 *The Guardian*, 19 September 1996.
91 K Marx and F Engels, *The German Ideology* (London, 1974), p55.

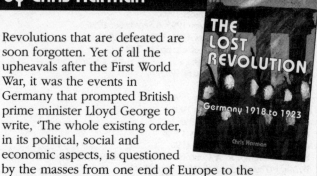

No more heroes: Nicaragua 1996

MIKE GONZALEZ

Elections in the disaster zone

Daniel Ortega lost a presidential election for the second time in October 1996. His 38 percent of the vote was easily surpassed by the 51 percent won by the candidate of the Liberal Alliance, Arnaldo Alemán, ex-mayor of Managua and an unscrupulous right wing populist. Ortega's subsequent claims of electoral fraud no doubt had some element of truth; yet 80 percent of the eligible population cast their ballots, and their verdict was incontestable.

In the post-mortems that follow it will be tempting to explain the result by reference to a hostile media or the appalling material reality in which people live now. That argument will defeat its own purpose: surely in such circumstances a revolutionary alternative would attract more rather than fewer people. The objective conditions would seem to be ripe once again for major and drastic change; yet the ordinary Nicaraguans who sacrificed so much in defence of their revolution through the 1980s were not convinced that Ortega and the Sandinistas could offer them any kind of solution. The gulf between the high rhetoric of the revolutionary leaders and the reality those fine words obscured has become a yawning abyss.

The material realities of today's Nicaragua are harsh in the extreme. Some 60 percent of the population are unemployed; the majority of the rest are underemployed; the annual per capita income in the country has returned to its 1945 level. Some 50 percent of the population live in extreme poverty, and 70 percent live below an internationally acknowledged poverty line. Nicaragua's gross domestic product (GDP) (at $425 per capita) is one of the lowest in the Western hemisphere—and stands at approximately the same level as it did in 1966. In 1992 alone the consumption of basic goods and services fell by an additional 37.5 percent.[1] That explains the roving groups of young people begging or stealing in the streets. The infrastructure is visibly collapsing: inter-city highways go unrepaired; city streets are pitted with holes. The majority of Managua's population—some one third of whom are recent refugees from the vicious fighting of the end of the 1980s in the north—live in makeshift shacks by the roadside or on empty, dusty plots. Public health provision, which did improve through the previous decade, is now virtually non-existent. Education, which was free under the Sandinista government, is now only available at a fee—a minimum of 100 córdobas per month per child, or six days wages for a seasonal agricultural worker. Managua, which was once remarkably free of hard drugs, has now become the main distribution point in Central America for crack and cocaine.[2] On the land, the small and middle peasants who in many cases benefited from land reform policies in the early 1980s are now enslaved by debt and crippling repayment conditions. Many of them are awaiting the outcome of court cases or government decrees which could return their lands to their pre-1979 owners.

It is hard to imagine the depth of the social and economic collapse which Nicaragua suffered after 1990. The statistics are brutal enough—but the reality they coldly describe was even worse, because in addition to material distress, the workers and peasants of Nicaragua had to deal with a terrible disillusionment.

A calculated crisis

The essential thing to understand is that this crisis is not an accident or merely the result of incompetence or corruption. The poverty and social collapse visible to all are the results of a strategy imposed by the central financial institutions of the world market and known universally as 'structural adjustment'.[3] Behind the cold terminology of 'neo-liberalism' lie decisions and agreements whose effects are devastating. In the case of Nicaragua the agreements for Emergency Economic Recovery were forged during 1990, after the defeat of the Sandinista government in February that year. There is a debate about the reasons for that defeat,[4] but what is clear is that, while the sustained economic and military assault upon Nicaragua organised by the United States was continuing, the hope that this interminable and costly struggle could be won had largely disappeared. The economic siege had terrible effects. The military defence of the country absorbed almost 70 percent of the gross domestic product, while the cost in dead, wounded and displaced rose to extraordinary levels (the Contra war almost certainly cost 50,000 lives and 100,000 wounded by the end of 1989). Yet even that in itself was not explanation enough for the Sandinista defeat at the polls. Crucially, the government of the Sandinista National Liberation Front (FSLN) had compromised so many of the ideals of the revolution, had conceded so much to the middle classes, that the victory came to seem hardly worth the candle:

For they gave priority to strengthening alliances with employers' and landowners' groups at the expense of the organisational independence of the working masses, workers and peasants, and the maintenance of their living standards. It was these sectors who bore the brunt of the war effort, both in terms of physical participation in the conflict and of paying its socio-economic costs.[5]

When, in 1990, the US-backed right wing candidate Violeta Chamorro promised aid and financial support *and* an end to war, a weary Nicaraguan population gave her the majority. The promised US aid, of course, was minimal and tied to the general conditions imposed by financial agencies like the IMF which finally agreed to negotiate with Nicaragua only after the 1990 elections. At the end of that year, an emergency programme was agreed—but there were no special concessions for Nicaragua: the conditions attached to financial assistance from the IMF were implacable. The Nicaraguan economy must open itself to the world market, remove all restrictions on imports, and guarantee that funds and credits would be allocated only to the private productive sector. Public spending on health, education or other forms of social reconstruction could not come out of these investment funds. And it was an explicit condition of the agreement that health and education should no longer be provided free.[6]

Translated into real decisions, this meant that by 1992 the bulk of investment in agriculture, for example, (75 percent) went to the large private estates producing export goods, 25 percent went to small and medium farms also producing mainly for the export sector, while the co-operative sector of collective farms or nationalised lands received nothing. As a result 80 percent of agricultural production occurred within a private sector increasingly devoting its lands to the production of export crops. The picture is entirely typical—the policy is universally applied, but its real effects and implications are perhaps more visible and more brutal in Nicaragua than almost anywhere else. For, in addition, subsidies on products for internal consumption were removed. This hit the poorest sectors of the population, the bulk of whose food and other needs were provided for by local production, and who had nothing whatsoever to gain from the flood of imported consumer goods that entered an almost ruined Nicaragua after 1990. The peasant co-operatives—the poorest of all—were now forced to go to private banks, whose interest rates were the highest and whose conditions for loans were the most cruel. Their standard of living collapsed and in many cases they lost their land and returned to casual and/or seasonal labour. Those that held on to their land were forced to impose upon themselves the most exploitative conditions of life. In the towns and cities all the social indices exposed the depth of the social crisis: infant mortality rates returned to the level of the early 1950s; illiteracy began to rise exponentially as the newest generation of young Nicaraguans saw their school careers abruptly curtailed. Their parents (70 percent of whom were jobless or severely underemployed) could not afford the new school fees insisted on by the IMF. The IMF Emergency Plan specifically excluded infrastructural investment or the use of available funds for purposes of creating or sustaining public services. Thus an already poor system of sewage, roads, healthcare and education now had to cope without additional funds with the influx of refugees from war. Yet health expenditure between 1989 and 1992 *fell* by 68 percent! What few industrial jobs there were—and these were almost entirely in Managua—disappeared as local industry was destroyed virtually in a single year (1992) as locally manufactured products were driven off the market by the arrival in bulk of cheaper imports, particularly textiles. And it is particularly revealing to look at where this increase in imports occurred. If we take the 1989 import figure as the baseline of 100, then by 1992 consumer goods had reached 299 and intermediate goods 106, while agricultural goods stood at 23.8.[7] The figure for agriculture should be set against the fact that domestic food production fell dramatically in the same year.

A pattern clearly emerges. In a period when all social indices were deteriorating dramatically for the mass of the population, when actual hunger was increasing and public health provision plummeting, some Nicaraguans were enjoying the flood of new consumer goods. For not everyone suffered equally under the impact of the Emergency Plan. Managua in 1996 is desperately poor, yet scattered about the city are prosperous middle class enclaves where new restaurants have opened and the houses betray a high level of conspicuous consumption. They also carry the signs of a new growth industry—private security. Solid new metal fences surround every house; fierce dogs bark incessantly behind their gates; alarm boxes sit high and visibly on the walls. And armed security guards patrol the streets of the well off neighbourhoods.

In Nicaragua everyone has guns. Where the most basic necessities are often hard to find, weapons and drugs seem to circulate with ease. It is indicative of the breakdown of any form of effective social organisation;

testimony too, to what might be called the secularisation of the military. In a country whose population is even now only slightly over 4 million (and 45 percent of them are under 15 years old), some 200,000 people had access to arms through the 1980s, distributed among the 65,000 members of the Sandinista army, the possibly 15,000 heavily armed Contras, the 100,000 militia fighters (who had access to arms through the army), and the police. The Contras were formally demobilised after 1990, the Nicaraguan army reduced by two thirds and the militia dismantled; but young Nicaraguans are very quick to show the visitor the guns that they took with them. For many of them, on both sides of the struggle of the 1980s, Nicaragua under the government of Chamorro's UNO has brought bitter disappointment and an ill concealed anger. One of the very few examples of public spending for welfare purposes in the last six years occurred in 1992, when Chamorro took resources from the public purse to provide compensation for unemployed soldiers. In fact they were $1,000 loans, and when the government tried to claim them back two years later, the ex-Sandinista soldiers occupied the banks in their hundreds and destroyed all records of the loans.

But there were other ex-Sandinistas who remained in the hills, still armed and still fighting a mythical enemy; these were the *recompas*. The soldiers who had fought for the Contras, the army maintained and supported by Ronald Reagan, President of the United States, and described by him as 'the new Maquis', came down from the hills in expectation of their reward. After all, their leaders had returned triumphantly from Miami and were now in government and sharing in its very selective prosperity. Many of these wealthy capitalists had their lands returned to them, or received generous compensation—but not the cannon fodder on the ground. They returned to the same conditions that were faced by those they had fought so bitterly. Some of them too returned to the hills, calling themselves the *recontras*. With time most of those who remained in the hills became mere bandits, preying on the very people they were still claiming to represent.

The abyss between the leaders and the led

In the new Nicaragua of Chamorro, the Sandinistas now became a parliamentary opposition. Their supporters waited restlessly for a sign that it was time to mount mass resistance in the streets and the factories—to use the Sandinista army in defence of the people, to set in motion the network of organisations on the ground. What they received instead were messages of caution, reassurances that Chamorro in power was good for the Sandinistas, that it was best to forge an alliance with her against the (even) more reactionary elements of her coalition. The alliance between the bourgeoisie and the FSLN forged in the years after 1984 was clearly still in operation but had now moved to the right. Strikes in several Managua factories were stopped by the army and the police, both of which contained large sections of ex-Sandinistas. The army was demobilised but the military command, held *jointly* by Violeta Chamorro and Humberto Ortega, offered nothing beyond rhetoric to the young men and women who had been prepared to die for a cause. The policies of structural adjustment were now biting with a vengeance; yet the leadership of the masses was still counselling caution, restraining action, and more generally accepting the 'inescapable' need for austerity. For the workers and peasants of Nicaragua, this can only have confirmed their deepening disillusionment. And if they asked why their leaders led them only towards disaster, there could only be one answer that real experience could confirm. In the deepening divide between the beneficiaries and the victims of the new 'neo-liberal' economy, the FSLN leaders were themselves among the first group. Their role in parliament merely confirmed what was already known about their lifestyles (see below).

What was clear beyond denial was that a yawning gulf separated the leadership of the FSLN from the mass base who had made the insurrection and carried them to power. The full extent of that division was not immediately obvious in 1990. Or at least, it was not clear to those who relied for their understanding of the Nicaraguan Revolution on those outside commentators who had supported the FSLN leadership uncritically through the 1980s,[8] who had confidently predicted their overwhelming victory in 1990,[9] who created a new myth to explain their defeat, and who in 1996 were still presenting the FSLN to the world as the champions of revolutionary purity.[10] The persistence of the myth explains the surprise with which those same commentators have greeted the 1996 results; but it offers no real understanding of why it is that Daniel Ortega could not convince *Nicaraguans* of the validity of his credentials, despite the fact that he carried the banner of revolution on his campaign trail.

The Sandinistas, so the legend goes, were the organisers of the heroic struggle against the Somoza dictatorship and the authors of his overthrow in 1979. After that, the official biographies assert, the Sandinistas sustained a principled struggle throughout the 1980s for a new version of socialism, democratic and mass based, against US imperialism, and they held true to that body of revolutionary principles. How then to explain the electoral defeat? It was a combination of war weariness and imperialist lies, aided and abetted by the conspirators gathered around Oliver North and the enormous power of the US media, which could not be successfully contested by a small, weak country like Nicaragua.[11] Those left wing intellectuals in Europe and the United States who have colluded with the myth fell oddly silent during the next six years—though they allowed Daniel Ortega to resume his mythic stature when the 1996 elections came around.

The battle for the spoils

Between the elections of February 1990 and the transfer of power two months later, the mythology exploded in the most spectacular manner.[12] In Nicaragua they call it *la piñata*, after the hollow figure which is filled with sweets and presents for a child's birthday and then gradually broken apart by determined wallopings from blindfolded children with a stick. When the figure bursts, all the kids dive onto the fallen pile of gifts and fight to gather as much as they can into their party bags. In the aftermath of the election defeat, it was the resources of the state that were the object of this sustained pillage.

State-owned properties were passed into the hands of individual Sandinistas. Every movable piece of equipment was taken. State bank accounts were transformed into personal wealth. The full extent of the pillage is not known, nor can it be measured. But what is clear is that nearly every member of the Sandinista government took what he or she could get and that many leaders of the FSLN became extremely rich. The ex-commander of the armed forces, Humberto Ortega, owns a huge estate in Managua and an unspecified private fortune. Tomás Borge, the only living representative of the original FSLN, is an extremely wealthy man with properties in Nicaragua and elsewhere. Since then Borge has gained a new notoriety in Mexico, where he was paid a fortune to write a hagiographic biography of President Carlos Salinas de Gortari, whose privatisation of the Mexican economy brought unimaginable wealth to himself and his cronies. Salinas is implicated in corruption, embezzlement and murder—and now resides in Ireland, which has no extradition treaty with Mexico. His huge accumulation of wealth was his reward for imposing upon the Mexican working class the crippling demands of the neo-liberal market. Tomas Borge used his reputation to defend this international gangster. Yet Borge remains owner and editor of the Sandinista newspaper *Barricada*.

When the transition to the new government was completed, the plunder of the state had created, almost overnight, a new bourgeoisie of ex-bureaucrats, ex-ministers and aides, all members or supporters of the FSLN. They moved into their recently acquired properties in the fashionable (and safe) districts, where they were joined soon after by the returning members of the old bourgeoisie. These were the people who enjoyed the new imported consumer goods that flooded the Nicaraguan market. It was they who patronised the new restaurants and cafes, and who employed the private security firms.

There was not even a pretence that this would benefit the mass of Nicaraguans. On the contrary, it was barefaced and open pillage. As the Sandinistas said, they simply had not expected to lose power, or to lose the privileges that came with power. Under pressure a rattled Daniel Ortega snarled at reporters, 'Why should the rich, the *Somocistas*, the pro-imperialists be the only ones to have satellite dishes... We didn't fight so that people could live in misery...'[13] There was no suggestion from him that anyone else should share the luxurious mansion once owned by a wealthy *Somocista* of which he was now the sole owner!

Corruption had its causes in the material reality. It was the product of the ability of individuals to act in their own interest alone, the evidence of a complete and total lack of accountability or control from below. Both before and after 1990 the FSLN had acted wholly pragmatically, without reference to any tradition or strategic project for revolutionary transformation. The *piñata* was not the sudden act of madness, but the rational action of those for whom personal power has become the most important determinant of their actions. The tragic irony (and the point will be addressed again) is that their ability to act in that way arose largely out of an orchestrated campaign among their supporters to conceal and deny the class nature of their politics and the confusions and contradictions which resulted from it.[14]

The explanation is to be found in the nature of the FSLN itself, in its origins and in its conduct during the latter half of the 1980s. For it was in that period that the FSLN became disengaged from its political base and began actively to construct a common front with sections of the bourgeoisie—an alliance whose imperatives flew directly in the face of the revolution and all it claimed to stand for. The commentators from the developed world, looking in on their favourite revolution, may not have seen it—but it was clearly visible to the mass of Nicaraguans.

The external signs were always there—in an impoverished Managua full of buildings still unrestored after the 1972 earthquake there were elegant living areas and suburbs where many state bureaucrats lived. Even in 1982, while I was travelling on an overcrowded bus towards Masaya, the other passengers commented loudly on the convoy of Cherokees and black Cadillacs with smoked glass windows that swept past us—'those are the "comandantes", the leaders of the revolution', they shouted. Throughout the 1980s, as the supermarket shelves emptied and most people faced deepening hardship, US dollars circulated widely and for those who had them consumer goods could easily be bought in special shops or brought back from Honduras or Costa Rica. It wasn't far, if you had a car and a passport—if you had neither, they might as well have been on the moon. The state hospitals were deprived of even the most basic medicine and equipment. That there was a service at all was largely thanks to the selflessness and sacrifice of nurses, paramedics and volunteer doctors. Schools were absolutely basic, and depended on the same human resources for their survival, although there were model establishments in both sectors financed externally by friendly governments or non-governmental organisations (NGOs). But private medicine and private education were always available and well endowed.

The point is that resources were accessible to one class but not to another; and as the FSLN leadership devoted themselves to pursuing a front with the bourgeoisie, their exclusive availability was a condition of continuing dialogue—and the Sandinista leadership themselves, naturally enough, had access to all these facilities. One party I went to in 1982 was attended by several FSLN leaders. In the house where it was held, owned by a British FSLN supporter living in Managua, servants and cooks served the guests, while the party giver moved among us—in an olive green uniform.

As the decade wore on, the assault on Nicaragua intensified. Despite external pressure, Daniel Ortega was elected to the presidency in 1984 with a two thirds majority of the electorate. After that Ronald Reagan was determined to bring the Nicaraguan state to its knees by all and every means—political, economic and military. Honduras became a support base for a well trained, well fed and extremely well equipped Contra force whose infrastructure was hidden in the Honduran army. The aftermath of Contra attacks was always particularly horrible. They tended to mutilate their victims before or after murdering them in order to terrorise the others.

But another change of much more significance was taking place, largely unnoticed outside Nicaragua, where right wing paranoia about Nicaragua and the coming Central American revolution vied with an uncritical support from the left, for whom any criticism of the Sandinistas was tantamount to a betrayal of the people's cause. In 1987 the Sandinista leadership embarked on a second stage of negotiation for peace, meeting with elements of the Contra leadership and continuing a peace process begun at Esquipulas under the auspices of the Costa Rican president, Oscar Arias. This was the last phase in a sequence of negotiations and compromises, but they also confirmed the central truth about the nature of the Sandinista Revolution. It was a process led from the state by a political class which combined different sectors of the bourgeosie, the leading sectors of the FSLN and the commanders of the army. The political project was never at any point to develop a revolutionary movement of workers and peasants, but to construct a state capable of taking its place at the concert of nations. The expropriation of key sectors of the economy after 1979, for example, ceased six months after the fall of Somoza—at that point where the process might have begun to encroach upon the sectors of private capital that were not part of Somoza's ruling clique. Immediately thereafter the Nicaraguan state distanced itself from the increasingly radical political movements in neighbouring El Salvador in order to re-establish its external links with European social democracy and Latin American Christian Democracy. Already it was clear that the issue for the Sandinistas was one of territorial integrity and the construction of a modern state. That was what was meant when the FSLN leaders spoke of a 'revolution of a new type',[15] for this was a 'revolution' in which the interests of workers and peasants were systematically subordinated to those of the bourgeoisie as a whole. Where resistance did occur—the Fabritex factory in Managua was a very good example—it was the Sandinista state which stepped in to stop the strike and eject the leading trade union activists.

The legend of the FSLN represents the Nicaraguan Revolution as the realisation of a plan evolved and carried through by the FSLN. In fact the revolution began with a mass insurrection which was spontaneous in character. At the time that it began (February 1978), in the town of Masaya, the Sandinistas were divided into three mutually hostile groupings who were not communicating with one another at all. Camilo Ortega, youngest brother of Daniel, was sent to Masaya to try and establish a relationship with the insurrectionaries, but was killed there before he could do so. The military actions for which the FSLN became known in subsequent months were evidence of a lack of organic links with the popular movement rather than the reverse—for the concept of politics on which they rested combined armed propaganda with the formation of broad alliances within and outside the country, the former expressed in the Group of Twelve, drawing together a range of political forces in support of the FSLN, the latter, for example, in the long term relationship with the Mexican governing party, the PRI. The FSLN did assume the political leadership of the movement against Somoza, and was the only organised force in a position to do so. But it is worth remembering that at the very outset the FSLN, while seeking the support and recognition of the capitalist class inside and outside Nicaragua, was ruthless with its own youthful left wing (La Milpa and El Pueblo) and quick to suppress a section of the Sandinista support (the Bolshevik faction) which, while admittedly sectarian, was asking important and incisive questions about the revolution and its political character.

The search for increasingly broad alliances with the bourgeosie continued throughout the 1980s, culminating in Ortega's signature of an Accord with Violeta Chamorro one month after his 1990 election defeat—which the Marxist PRT described as a form of 'co-government'.[16] When, between 1984 and 1990, the mass of ordinary

Nicaraguans lived through hunger, violence and an inflation that reached over 60,000 percent in 1988, the FSLN argued fiercely that sacrifice and scarcity were the conditions of survival. But it was certainly not the case for everyone. The FSLN's political allies were protected from the social costs—it was the fundamental price of negotiation. The much vaunted process of reconciliation was not concerned with the mass of Nicaraguan workers and peasants, whose living standards were collapsing by the month, whose sons and daughters were dying at the front. But it did involve frequent journeys by leading Sandinistas to Mexico, Venezuela, Britain and Spain seeking allies with their repeated reassurances that the FSLN was committed to a mixed economy and was prepared to devolve property *back* to the private sector. As a gesture of goodwill, it even announced an amnesty for ex-*Somocista* National Guards, many of them fighting and murdering peasants still.

The introduction of conscription in 1989 was not merely an error, therefore. It was an indication of the relationship between the state and the social base of the revolution. The Nicaraguan state was administering an austerity programme at the expense of the masses; and it was secretly negotiating with the bourgeois opposition as it did so. It is hardly surprising that it lost the confidence of a significant section among its old supporters, who in 1990 opted for what they imagined would be some kind of economic recovery and an end to war *because they were offered no political alternative*. The state was run by functionaries. There was no long term political or economic project to adhere to, no principle at work in the conduct of daily life. The Sandinista leaders were nominees of a tiny group, unaccountable and without allegiances, individuals in pursuit of power and wealth. That is why they pillaged everything.

Two and three years later these were the people buying the imported luxury goods, enjoying the fruits of external credit, acting for foreign companies and agencies. One of them was Arnaldo Aleman,[17] who became the UNO's mayor of Managua. He cleaned the streets and built public works projects. It meant no improvement in the life of any inhabitant of the capital, but it was something! And he attacked both the Sandinistas and UNO, whose leader, Violeta Chamorro, he accused of being in league with the Communists (oddly, both Nicaraguan Communist parties were members of the UNO coalition).

The irony, of course, was that there was a germ of truth in what he said. The Sandinistas were arguing, *against* their own supporters, that the Chamorro government should be kept in power because the alternative power blocs waiting in the wings would be even more ruthless. It is hard to imagine any group imposing economic policies whose effects could have been more devastating. Yet Ortega and the majority of FSLN argued against social agitation, strikes or public demonstrations because they would 'fuel the right'. In other words, the pre-1990 coalition continued in power, and defended what must rank as one of the most inhuman applications of economic strategy that we can point to. For six years the Sandinistas defended this Nicaraguan democracy which had wreaked such havoc amongst the majority. They argued that, if social peace were maintained, the Sandinistas would return to power in 1996.

But what could Nicaragua expect of the FSLN in power? The answer was given long before the votes were cast. Through six years they argued that the austerity plan and structural adjustment were necessary. They defended the Chamorro regime. They collaborated with it in all its phases, and oversaw the destruction of those few gains the mass of the people had made under the Sandinista government. Their leaders (with one honourable exception, 'Modesto', Henry Ruiz) grew rich and powerful. Ortega shed his uniform as the election campaign began for the jeans and baseball cap of the career politician. Both he and Tomás Borge were photographed in the weeks prior to the election shaking hands with Cardinal Obando y Bravo, leader throughout the 1980s of the bourgeois opposition to *Sandinismo* and scourge of the left wing Catholics who had played such an important role in mobilising popular opinion behind the revolution. Consensus, it seemed, would be built with such people as these, or the ex-Contras to whom the FSLN had already promised three key ministries in any future government.

The role of the cheerleaders

In preparation for the elections, the British Nicaragua Solidarity Campaign issued a leaflet calling for support for the Sandinistas abroad. A vote for the FSLN, it claimed, was 'a vote for those who have the interests of the poor at heart'. The record of the Sandinistas in power shows that their primary concern was a defence of the Sandinista state rather than the interests of the poor, which they were willing to sacrifice to the political alliance with the bourgeoisie. The record of the Sandinistas out of power shows a continuation of that alliance, and a readiness to use the authority of the Nicaraguan Revolution to hold back the class struggle. Why? The principal consideration was to win the 1996 elections, even if that meant creating an even more wide ranging set of coalitions and pacifying their own working class supporters in order to present a respectable face to world opinion. Yet the Sandinistas still depended for victory on a strong and permanent base among Nicaraguans who by and large have clearly seen how little they can rely on the leadership of the FSLN.

What then could induce sincere socialists and liberals outside

Nicaragua to argue in their favour? Why do they agree to suppress the truth about *la piñata*, the personal corruption of the Sandinista leadership, the FSLN's collusion with Chamorro throughout the six years of her presidency, the gulf between the Sandinista leadership and its base? In February the Pope visited Nicaragua. The road he travelled was newly painted, street lighting recently installed and pavements laid. All these renovations stopped abruptly half way into the city—at the point where the Pope's cavalcade would turn around and return to the airport. Where were the Sandinista protests, the demonstrations, the denunciations? There were none, only a handshake with the cardinal.

Despite their best intentions the activists who suppress these truths are colluding in a confidence trick. The implication is that the only alternative available for socialists is a choice between political cliques vying for power in a system whose codes of conduct and prevailing economic imperatives they accept. The fine poetic speeches of Tomás Borge produce only hollow laughter among many Mexican workers. Ortega's expressions of Sandinista 'orthodoxy' mean very little when his concerns are to seek his allies among sections of the bourgeoisie. To argue that these people are the appropriate representatives of the mass of Nicaraguans is more than an expression of the most extreme historical pessimism—it is an explicit rejection of the premise that the working class is the instrument of its own liberation.

The paradox is that many of the features that have created confusion and disorientation among those Nicaraguan workers and peasants who *did* make the revolution have been celebrated by the FSLN's admirers abroad. Its ideological confusion has been transformed into openness and flexibility. Its lack of any strategic direction for the revolutionary transformation of society has become an admirable pragmatism, its profoundly militaristic rhetoric allowed to hide the command vision of political organisation which has deprived the Nicaraguan workers of any democratic control over their own political destiny.

When 19 candidates presented themselves in the October 1996 presidential elections, it was not a sign of a vigorous democracy but evidence that political power was once again being fought for by small cliques battling with one another. The split within the Sandinistas, when ex Vice-President Sergio Ramírez formed his own Sandinista Renewal Movement (MRS), did not indicate a break to the left. Ramirez was interested in creating an explicitly social democratic organisation. In the elections it achieved less than 1 percent of the vote. Daniel Ortega, on the other hand, described himself and his followers as *'los ortodoxos'*— the orthodox Sandinistas—in the hope that he could mobilise behind his own campaign the loyalty that many people still feel towards the revolution and the aspirations still expressed, for some people, in the idea of

Sandinismo.

The high percentage of Nicaraguans voting (80 percent) bears witness to a desire for involvement, a yearning for change and some improvement in people's lives. But in every real sense the mass of ordinary Nicaraguans were mere spectators at the feast. There was very little in this electoral process to give them hope. As always, the real class struggle is conducted elsewhere. While the politicians vie for their share of the booty, the concrete reality of daily life has once again begun to generate resistance among those people who did fight the Nicaraguan Revolution of 1978-1979.

In towns like Esteli in the north, new organisations are emerging from the day to day struggles. Significantly the *Movimiento Comunitario*, formed about two years ago, sets out to link and lead those struggles on the ground. It embraces people who not very long ago were fighting each other in the Sandinista and the Contra armies—and who share both a common misery and a deep disillusionment with their old leaders. They are open to all sorts of ideological influences—evangelical groups are proliferating with astonishing speed in Central America for example. But they are also the soil in which revolutionary ideas can grow, if those ideas are present in their struggles. A revolutionary understanding, however, is not an abstraction, the fruit of mere theoretical purification. It grows out of a critical approach to the real history of the struggle. In Nicaragua, for example, the first step must be to honestly confront the way in which the revolutionary impulse has been distorted and misused, and to address the true history of *Sandinismo*. To evade the responsibility which falls on all socialists to recognise what has happened in Nicaragua may win approval from the FSLN leadership—but it will contribute nothing to the rebirth of revolution in this 'region of storms'.

Notes

1   See *Latin America Weekly Report*, 28 December 1995, and A J A Vogl, *Nicaragua y el FMI* (Managua, 1993), pp7-12.

2   There are clear links here between the distribution of drugs and US government and CIA involvement in Central America: see *Guardian Weekend*, 19 November 1996, pp4-5.

3   See D Green, *The Silent Revolution* (London, 1996), especially ch 1.

4   See M. Gonzalez, *Nicaragua: What Went Wrong?* (Bookmarks, 1990). See also C Vilas, 'Nicaragua a Revolution that Fell from Grace of the People', *Socialist Register 1991* (Merlin Books, 1991),pp 303-321.

5   C Vilas, op cit p303. Carlos Vilas wrote regularly on the development of the Nicaraguan process; for example in C Vilas and R Harris (eds), *Nicaragua: Revolution Under Siege* (Zed Books, 1985), and in articles in *Socialist Register* through the 1980s.

6   A Vogl, op cit, pp21-38.

7   Ibid, p93.

8   The bibliography in this regard is enormous. Inspired by the optimism that grew out of the overthrow of Somoza by a mass insurrectionary movement, and of a resolute and incontestable anti-imperialism, foreign commentators were largely responsible for rewriting Nicaragua's history to locate the FSLN in a commanding central role—in retrospect—and later for colluding in a denial of the direction that was taken by the FSLN leadership itself. One example is George Black's history of the Nicaraguan Revolution, *Triumph of the People* (London, 1982).

9   For example, Alexander Chancellor's article, 'Uncle Sam's Dirty War', *Guardian Weekend*, 10-11 Feburary 1990, pp4-6, in which the subheading asserts 'Washington's Power Brokers Face Another Humiliation at the Hands of Ortega's Sandinistas'.

10   See, for example, the leaflet issued by the British Nicaragua Solidarity Campaign for the 1996 elections.

11   The question of the media, and in particular the body of analytical writing by Noam Chomsky on the role and power of the US media in sabotaging democratic projects in Latin America, is by no means a simple one. There can be no denying the conscious use of the media as instruments of disinformation—and their willing collusion in that role. The discovery of Russian Mig fighters emblazoned across all the US media before the elections of 1984 were cheerfully acknowledged as completely spurious a year later, for example. Yet Chomsky's assertion of their extraordinary power yields deeply pessimistic conclusions as well as providing an alibi too conveniently seized upon to mask the absence of an effective political strategy. In a word, they are powerful, but not all-powerful.

12   See J Castañeda, *La Utopía Desarmada* (Mexico, 1993), p411. Also M Walker, 'Sandinistas in Search of a Fresh Role' in *The Guardian*, 9 March 1990, p11.

13   Quoted in J Castañeda, op cit, p412 fn.

14   It is appropriate to point out that this is not wisdom after the event. This journal, along with other Socialist Workers Party publications, has consistently pointed to the opportunism of the FSLN, its lack of any organic or political link to the revolutionary working class tradition, and to the substitution of the leaders for the class that is so deeply embedded in the guerrilla war tradition from which the FSLN emerged. See for, example, M Gonzalez, op cit.

15   In *Fire Over the Americas* (Verso, 1987) Roger Orbach and Carlos Núñez formulated the case for a politics of 'the third way'. But, fiery rhetoric apart, it ploughed a very familiar furrow, recasting the argument for a 'popular front' in new forms. In any event, the publication of the book coincided precisely with new compromises with the Contras which rendered most of its ringing declarations meaningless.

16   See *Latin America Weekly Report*, 5 April 1990.

17   See M Caster, 'The Return of Somocismo?' in *NACLA Report on the Americas* XXX/2 September/October 1996, pp6-9.

Tumults and commotions: turning the world upside down

A review of David Underdown, **A Freeborn People: Politics and the Nation in 17th Century England** *(Oxford University Press, 1996), £25*

CHRISTOPHER HILL

David Underdown's Ford Lectures of 1992 make a challenging book. Historians have come to accept that what used to be called 'the Puritan Revolution' in England was not, in fact, about theology but was the first of the great political revolutions which ushered in the modern world. It set the example for the American, French and Russian revolutions which followed. Historians have not yet properly distinguished the social and political causes of the English Revolution, or recognised the precise distinctions to be drawn between 'the politics of the elite' and 'the politics of the people'.

In the English Revolution the gentry were concerned primarily with government, bureaucracy and state-building; a less propertied section of 'the political nation' was trying to preserve its version of the 'Ancient Constitution', and to defend both local and national rights against the encroaching central state and the excesses of acquisitive individualism. 'Popular politics was conservative but by no means universally deferential'.[1]

Underdown asks why, after the dramatic scenes preceding the dissolution of parliament in 1629, Charles I's personal rule should have roused so little open opposition in the early 1630s, despite talk of a 'sinister popish plot against England's liberty and independence'.[2] The gentry still accepted the monarch, and some of them felt that MPs 'itching after popularity' had gone too far in 1628-1629, giving rise to popular discontent outside parliament. Experience of the civil war led Sir

Robert Filmer to write *Patriarcha* by 1632, to defend the 'Natural Power of Kings against the Unnatural Liberty of the People'.[3] *Patriarcha* circulated in manuscript form, though it was not published until 1680.

The gentry had traditionally taken the lead in protests against oppressive or illegal taxes, but—as an MP had observed—such taxes always 'bred tumults and commotions'. By 1639 people were refusing to pay Ship Money, boycotting auctions of distrained cattle and rescuing constables who had been arrested for refusing to co-operate. 'Even the bravest constable', a high sheriff ruefully admitted, 'dare do nothing but what the parish allow of'.[4] Experience of civil war convinced the gentry that putting arms into the hands of the common people was too dangerous. 'Liberty and property', 'church and king' became the slogans of propertied Englishmen for the next century.[5]

Certain aspects of what was a common culture seem to have been stressed more strongly at the popular than at the elite level—notably those connected with issues of gender of inversion. Underdown reminds us of the literary controversy started by Joseph Swetman's *Arraignment of Lewd, Idle, Forward and Unconstant Women* in 1615, attacking the masculine style which women were adopting, and the effeminacy in both dress and behaviour of some courtiers, including, perhaps, James I himself.[6]

Underdown examines *The Man in the Moon*, a scandalmongering royalist weekly edited by John Crouch from April 1649 to June 1650.[7] Frivolous and pornographic, and selling for 1d, the periodical had a large potential readership. It upheld a very traditional moral order. Its instances of sexual transgression nearly always involved hypocritical Puritans and, significantly, women who rebelled against masculine authority. 'The words "freedom and liberty", so prominent in rebel rhetoric, became in Crouch's paper merely passwords for entering brothels patronised by leading Parliament men'.[8]

The murder of the king, Crouch insisted, was inevitably accompanied by 'a chaos of sects and schisms, heresies and blasphemies, openly tolerated and taught, nay protected by these regicides'.[9] 'Central to Crouch's condemnation of the regicides', Underdown comments, 'is his contention that they are violating liberties protected by the Ancient Constitution, in ways that the King at his worst had never done'. Parliament's excise on food and drink was 'far more oppressive than Charles I's Ship Money had been'.[10]

'The inversion of government was accompanied by sexual inversion'— and by inversion of the natural order in family, social relations and the church. Quakers exemplified this by giving unprecedented freedom to women. 'Mob violence against women was often provoked by their rejection of distinctions of gender and rank'.[11] Witchcraft accusations were levelled at both male and female Quakers. 'Witchcraft beliefs, with their underlying identification of disorder with unruly women, were held as strongly by educated people as by their inferiors'.[12] Masculine women were routinely linked with witchcraft. Crouch in 1654 promised to write:

Of hags and cats, of imps and witches,
Of man-kind women that wear britches. [13]

Underdown concludes that 'gentry and plebians shared many elements of a common political language...based on a widespread acceptance of theories of partriarchal authority in the family, hierarchical authority in the community, and legitimate monarchical authority in the state'—all bound by law and custom. But he also notes:

...the division between the elite and the populace...is surely the most striking change in the political nation during the 17th century. The country had been relatively united before 1640, in opposition to both religious and constitutional innovation.[14]

His final words are:

We have heard a lot recently about clientage and deference in the 17th and 18th centuries. Important as those notions undoubtedly were, it does us no harm, I think, to remind ourselves that both branches of the political nation were inspired by other ideas as well; by ideas stemming from the myth of the Ancient Constitution... Embedded in the vocabulary of law and liberty that survived in the gentry's political culture was the concept, which when they were honest about it, extended even to the poorest vagrant, of the freeborn people of England.[15]

Without any fuss, Underdown has given historians a lot to think about. My only query, as devil's advocate, would be to ask—how often were the gentry honest about it? Not 'some benevolent gentlemen' but 'the gentry'?

Notes

1   D Underdown, *A Freeborn People: Politics and the Nation in 17th Century England* (Oxford University Press, 1996), ppvi-viii.
2   Ibid, p42.
3   Ibid, p44.
4   Ibid, p53.
5   Ibid, p89.
6   Ibid, pp64-67.

7   Ibid, pp95-98.
8   Ibid, p103.
9   Ibid, p105.
10 Ibid, p108.
11 Ibid, pp104-105.
12 Ibid, p129.
13 Ibid, p107.
14 Ibid, p128.
15 Ibid, pp131-132.

Capitalism without frontiers?

A review of Nigel Harris, **The New Untouchables—Immigration and the New World Worker** *(IB Tauris, 1995), £25 hb/£8.99 pb*

PETER MORGAN

Towards the end of his new book on immigration, Nigel Harris gives the following definition of 'globalisation':

> *Global integration is making the movement of commodities, of finance and of workers, greater and greater—movement increases faster than output. The world economy, it seems, has by now passed the point of no return, and we are set upon the road to a single integrated global economy, regardless of the wishes of governments and citizens. Indeed, any efforts to reverse the process, spell catastrophe.*[1]

It is true that one of the tasks that governments throughout the world set themselves in the 1980s was the ability to move huge sums of money and capital at speeds not imaginable in the past—deregulation of the financial markets, combined with enormous advances in technology made this possible. But there is, however, one problem in all this. Why is it that the so-called globalisation and integration of the world's economy has gone hand in hand with greater restrictions in the movement of the world's population? Why is it that such enormous numbers of the world's population are subject to even more stringent and draconian controls? Unfortunately this is the question that Nigel Harris is not able to answer in his new book.

Europe provides a good example of how both processes develop simultaneously. On the one hand there is the attempt to move towards greater integration between the European economies. This is what lies behind the whole EMU project—the lowering of restrictions between the various European economies, convergence of the currencies, greater political co-operation, and supposedly, the free movement of labour between member states—globalisation, if you like, on a smaller scale. But this is fraught with tensions, splits and fallouts as each government's overriding concern with its national economy often brings it into conflict with the need for greater European integration. This has also gone hand in hand with the European governments becoming less hospitable to migrants and asylum seekers.

In Britain, the Tory government passed the 1995 Immigration and Asylum Act making it even harder for those fleeing persecution and repression overseas to enter Britain. The Italian government recently passed a decree making it easier for them to expel immigrants, Holland has brought its law into line with other countries and allows virtually no new immigrants, and Germany has spent the last few years trying to plug the gaps in its once 'liberal' immigration laws. And all the European Union's members recently agreed to narrow the definition of who may qualify for asylum. This poses the question of why, as the world economy supposedly becomes more integrated, the ruling governments feel compelled to be more repressive.

In one of the stronger sections of Harris's book, he makes it clear that migration is nothing new to the capitalist system. Indeed the great economies of the world have been built by migrant labour. Between 10 million and 20 million Africans were forced to cross the Atlantic and work the plantations of America, and 'possibly some 50 million Indians and Chinese (between 1840 and 1930) were recruited by the gangsters of empire for work in California, Southeast Asia and Africa'.[2] And even in Europe the demand for labour from countries outside the region was necessary for economic growth. As Harris observes:

> ...the historical record would suggest that any reasonable level of economic growth in Europe would lead to labour demand exceeding local supply. Far from Europe being sharply distinguished from the Americas—the so-called 'countries of immigration'—all advanced industrialising powers required immigration to sustain growth...it is important not to forget that immigration is by no means a modern phenomenon. Everyone in Europe is ultimately descended from immigrants, some more recently than others.[3]

The movement of large sections of the world's population is a peculiar feature of the capitalist system, and people will always endeavour to seek jobs and a better standard of living despite the restrictions and boundaries that are placed in their way. As Eric Hobsbawm notes, the middle of the 19th century marked the beginning of the greatest migration of peoples in history, and it was not merely from one country to the next, but rather it was, as he says:

> the rural exodus towards the cities, the migration between regions and from town to town, the crossing of oceans and the penetration of frontier zones, the flux of men and women moving back and forth... Population movements and industrialisation go together, for the modern economic development of the world both required substantial shifts of people, made it technically easier and cheaper by means of new and improved communications, and of course enabled the world to maintain a much larger population.[4]

By the mid-1800s an annual average of approximately 250,000 people left Europe each year. But however enormous this was, it was modest compared to what was to come: in the 1880s between 700,000 and 800,000 Europeans migrated each year and in the years just after 1900 it was between 1 million and 1.4 million.[5] This went hand in hand with the movement of people from the country to the city—migration and urbanisation went together. In the second half of the 19th century those countries chiefly associated with migration (the US, Australia, Argentina) had a rate of urban concentration unsurpassed anywhere except in Britain and the industrial parts of Germany.

Today there are still large sections of the world's economy that are heavily dependent on migrant labour. As the *Far Eastern Economic Review* said, 'Malaysia is now home to almost 1 million foreign workers; tiny Hong Kong has more than 100,000 maids from Southeast Asia; and within China there exists a floating population of up to 150 million people, 10 million of whom are now an integral part of the Guangdong economy'.[6] And one of the strengths of Harris's book is the wealth of statistical detail on the movement of labour, particularly during this century, and the way in which governments have encouraged such movements. He gives the example of the Philippines which, by the early 1990s, was the second biggest exporter of labour (after Mexico), with some 600,000 leaving annually, predominantly to be employed as seamen, nurses or domestic labour. This movement was encouraged by the Philippine government. In 1975 President Marcos established a policy of promoting work abroad with the intention of forcing the migrants to return a proportion of their income to bank accounts in the Philippines. This led to an explosion of illegal recruitment agencies promoting the availability of Philippine labour overseas, often at appalling rates of pay.

Today Asian women are the fastest growing group of migrant workers in the world (and one of the most exploited and abused). According to the International Labour Organisation about 1.5 million Asian women are working abroad, many in slave-like conditions in domestic service or the 'entertainment' industry. Further illegal migration, often through well organised and underground syndicates, is estimated to account for well over half of the total migration flows in some countries. The ILO states that, 'were it not for illegal recruitment agencies, overseas employment promoters, manpower suppliers and a host of other legal and illegal subsidiaries, Asian labour migration would not have reached such a massive scale'.[7]

But if immigration is so central to the workings of capitalism, what is the logic for an increase in immigration controls? At times of economic boom, there are few or no restrictions on immigration. Indeed, governments actively encourage migration. This was particularly the case following the end of the Second World War in Britain. A report in 1949 from the Royal Commission on Population recommended that immigration into Britain should be encouraged, and British employers were pleased to welcome Indian and Caribbean workers. The problems arise, however, when the economy goes into recession, as it did in Britain in the 1970s. Prior to then bosses had a pool of labour who lived in other parts of the world and were encouraged, often financially, to move to Britain. But with the onset of recession and the accompanying rise in unemployment, they were able to call upon an excess pool of labour which existed in the home country without the inconvenience of importing migrants who could then become a problem the government no longer needed, and no longer wanted to support. So their entry was increasingly restricted, by both Tory and Labour governments.

Harris looks at the restrictions on migrants purely in terms of the capitalist system as a whole and he concludes that they have no logic either during times of boom or during recession. He presents a convincing body of argument against those who favour greater restriction. Firstly, it is not true that increased immigration leads to increased unemployment. Harris quotes Borjas, who argues that 'modern econometrics cannot find a single shred of evidence that immigrants have an adverse impact on the earnings and job opportunities of natives of the United States'.[8] And he gives the example of the Los Angeles economy which expanded in the 1970s, largely as the result of increased demand caused by legal and illegal immigration. Likewise the increase in immigration in Britain in the 1950s and 1960s did not lead to increased unemployment—rather the massive explosion in unemployment levels in the 1970s and beyond was caused by the boom-bust cycle of the capitalist system itself.

Secondly, immigrants and refugees are not a drain on the social security system—in fact, as Harris shows, they contribute far more to the 'system' than they receive in return. Whether you look at Caribbean immigrants who came to Britain in the 1960s, few of which drew retirement pensions, or whether you take Mexican migrants to California, where a 1980 study found that less than 5 percent received any assistance from welfare services, and in all sectors, except education, they paid far more than they received—a net balance sheet shows that the 'host' nation gains far more than it gives in return. Furthermore, migration has another very favourable benefit for the ruling class in the 'host' country—namely that they don't have to contribute to the cost of raising and educating the immigrant worker.

But reiterating the logical economic argument does not help explain why restrictions on the movement of labour are still in place, and are becoming more draconian. In order to square the circle, Harris argues that we are moving to a global economy in which increased movement of both commodities and labour will become unhindered:

The idea that people of necessity are permanently located in one national entity is also under challenge. World economic integration continually increases rates of mobility, so that in the future it is going to be as difficult internationally to give an unequivocal answer to the question 'Where are you from?' as it already is in developed countries. Native places are in decline and often the complex of origins is well beyond the conventional mythology. The marks of identity may remain individual, ancestral, tribal, occupational—and even religious—rather than national.[9]

He bases this assumption on the argument that the nation state is disappearing as the economic imperatives of the market and globalisation force greater integration and co-operation: '...these processes will lead to the creation of a single integrated global economy with geographically diversified sources of growth...[and] as governments have been driven, to different degrees, to end the old social contract with their citizens, to dismantle the socialised state, so has the emergence of global labour markets made for continuously increasing rates of worker mobility'.[10]

In reality, however, the functions of the state are not dwindling. On the contrary, what characterises late 20th century capitalism is both the political and economic importance of the state in defending and supporting 'their' own capitalist interests. Chris Harman in the last issue of *International Socialism* (No 73) attacked the globalisation thesis that assumes firms are becoming increasingly independent from their 'home' states. He draws on the work of Paul Hirst and Grahame Thompson who demonstrate that there are limits to the extent that so-called globalisation has taken place. They show how the multinationals that dominate the global economy today are still 'tied' and dependent upon their 'own' nation state and its market for their trade and profits:

> *The home oriented nature of MNC* [multinational corporation] *activity...*
> *seems overwhelming. Thus MNC's still rely upon their 'home base' as the*
> *centre for their economic activities, despite all the speculation about globali-*
> *sation...*[and] *it would not seem unreasonable to suggest that between 70 and*
> *75 percent of MNC value added was produced in the home territory.*[11]

For American multinationals, 64 percent of manufacturing sales and
75 percent of service sales are to the home market. For Japanese multinationals it is 75 percent of manufacturing and 77 percent for services.
And a look at the assets of these companies shows that they are similarly
concentrated in their 'own' economy. Both US and Japanese multinational corporations have the majority of their assets concentrated at
'home', and for European countries the picture is the same if Europe as a
whole is considered the home region.

Capitalism needs states—to regulate relations between firms, sometimes by the use of violence; to impose common laws and currency
which aid capital accumulation; to organise labour markets and the provision of education, transport and healthcare and to try to prevent
recession turning into economic collapse. In fact the deeper the crisis, the
greater the tensions between firms, the more the competition heats up,
the more the state is needed to impose some sort of 'order'. So today, far
from the state disappearing, it plays an increasingly important function
in the regulation of the world economy such as we see in Europe and the
EMU.

However, Harris is unable to come to terms with a crucial fact—that
the state also has a role to play in aiding and assisting in the exploitation
of the workforce—hence the use of immigration controls and racism. On
the one hand those who own and control the wealth want the freedom to
make as much profit whenever and however they want. But at the same
time the system is based on oppression and exploitation, so they demand
the right to restrict the freedom and movement of labour. These restrictions take the form both of attacking trade unions at 'home', and also
controlling those that are forced to move abroad. In a crisis ridden
system this has a logic that is both economic *and political*—immigration
controls lead to racism which increases divisions and facilitates greater
exploitation. Indeed the attempt to create and perpetuate racist divisions
within the working class has always been an essential feature of the capitalist system. This was a point that Marx recognised over 100 years ago
when he talked about the racism directed by English workers against
migrant Irish workers. He called this antagonism the 'secret of the impo-
tence of the English working class... It is the secret by which the
capitalist class maintains its power.'

Because Harris overstates the case for globalisation, or the shift from
what he calls 'semi-closed' national economies to an open world

economy, this has all sorts of implications for how he sees the 'irrationality' of immigration controls. Firstly he concludes that we are heading towards the end to the wars 'which were the product of the heyday of national egotism', a conclusion that does not fit well with the fact that war deaths have increased since 1989 or a comparison of the period since the Second World War with the previous 'peacetime' period, the inter-war years. Secondly he suggests that the increased movement of labour can be regulated by an international forum:

> *where governments negotiate—as they do in GATT and now the World Trade Organisation, mutual concessions on the restrictions to movement—a General Agreement on Migration and Refugee Policy. Such a forum could provide a body capable of reprimanding governments which seek to use resident foreigners as scapegoats for domestic discontents or cat-paws in their foreign policy.*[12]

But the GATT agreement was concerned with the main capitalist countries' increasing exploitation of the 'developing' economies and is a symbol of everything that is rotten about the capitalist system. The 20th century has been characterised by the bosses setting up organisations and agreements to try and regulate the problems of the system—such as the League of Nations, the Dollar Standard, the IMF, the World Bank or the United Nations, or the G7 economic summits. And each time the attempt has resulted in a breakdown of agreements and more conflict between the various powers as the interests of each state conflicts with others and the needs of the system as a whole. The breakdown either results in war, or in deeper recessions and a more prolonged crisis. The idea that the ruling class would come to some sort of agreement or create a body that would represent the interests of labour (migrants) instead of capital, flies in the face of all historical empirical evidence (all the more surprising when you find that earlier in the book Harris goes to great lengths to go through the various restrictions and legislation that have been passed by various capitalist governments against immigrants during the 20th century).

Harris therefore has to reconcile his argument that we have an antiquated system of nation states being replaced by greater globalisation, with the fact that an increase in the movement of labour is being hindered by illogical and outdated restrictions. This he does by calling for a new 'world morality and a world system of law', or 'a new universal morality—like Hegel's Spirit of Reason', which he says are 'struggling to be reborn after the long dark night of nationalism'.[13]

Instead it is important to reassert the point that the nation state is not some outdated relic from the past that has outlived its usefulness. Rather it plays a very specific function in the modern capitalist economy with regard to migrants—regulating their movement, creating divisions and increasing exploitation. As the problems of the modern global capitalist economy become more acute, as the gulf between rich and poor becomes greater so too will the desire of the capitalist class to use all weapons—in particular that of racism—to divide working people. The response is not to hope that some 'universal morality' will prevail, rather it is to fight for the common interest of working class unity.

Notes

1   N Harris, *The New Untouchables* (I B Tauris, 1995), p226.
2   Ibid, p3.
3   Ibid, p3.
4   E Hobsbawm, *The Age of Capital 1848-1875* (Abacus, London, 1995), p228.
5   Ibid, p229.
6   'Room at the Inn', *Far Eastern Economic Review*, 29 December 1994 and 5 January 1995, p5.
7   L Lim and N Oishi, 'International Labour Migration of Asian women: Distinctive Characteristics and Policy Concerns' (International Labour Organisation), 1996.
8   N Harris, op cit, p194.
9   Ibid, p217.
10   Ibid, p216.
11   P Hirst and G Thompson, *Globalisation in Question* (Polity, 1996), pp96-97.
12   N Harris, op cit, p224.
13   Ibid, p228.

Minds, machines and evolution: a reply to John Parrington and Joe Faith

ALEX CALLINICOS

In one of the most interesting passages of his *Philosophical Notebooks* Trotsky confronts what philosophers call the mind-body problem. For materialists this takes the form of the question of how physical organisms like us can generate the complex and interrelated array of mental states that constitutes human consciousness. Trotsky rules out a reductionist solution to this problem which treats the mind (or psyche) as a mere epiphenomenon, a passive effect, of the body:

> By itself the method of psychoanalysis, taking as its point of departure 'the autonomy' of psychological phenomena, in no way contradicts materialism. Quite on the contrary, it is precisely dialectical materialism that prompts us to the idea that the psyche could not even be formed unless it played an autonomous, that is, within certain limits, an independent role in the life of the individual and the species.
>
> All the same, we approach here some sort of critical point, a break in the gradualness, a transition from quantity to quality: the psyche, arising from matter, is 'freed' from the determinism of matter, so that it can—by its own laws—influence matter.[1]

Trotsky goes on to point to the analogy between the interaction of mind and body and the way in which, in human history, the ideological and political superstructure arises out of the economic base but reacts back on it. He nevertheless admits 'When we make the transition from the anatomy and physiology of the brain to intellectual activity, the interrela tionship of "base" to "superstructure" is incomparably more puzzling.'[2]

Trotsky is right. The mind-body problem is one of the most difficult in philosophy. When grappling with it, theorists are constantly liable to one of two errors. They can, in the first place, collapse into mechanical materialism, treating mental states as somehow directly correlated with physical events, and thereby denying what Trotsky calls '"the autonomy" of psychological phenomena'. This error is mirrored by a second—idealism—which treats mental and physical events as absolutely different, and so transforms the mind into a mysterious phenomenon unamenable to scientific explanation.

Marxists are not immune from either of these mistakes. In fact, in their replies to my review article of the American philosopher Daniel Dennett's book *Darwin's Dangerous Idea*, both John Parrington and Joe Faith generally show a slight tendency in the idealist direction.[3] They are, however, concerned to correct what they appear to regard as a serious lapse into mechanical materialism on my part, reflected particularly in my relatively friendly treatment of Dennett's philosophy of mind.

It may be helpful for me, before going on to consider John's and Joe's criticisms in a little detail, to make three general points about this treatment. First, despite the fact that Dennett's book is about Darwin's theory of evolution, it seemed to me unavoidable to discuss the former's philosophy of mind. One of Dennett's purposes in *Darwin's Dangerous Idea* was evidently to use evolutionary theory as a way of attacking the problem that preoccupied his earlier philosophical writings, namely that of how human mental life could emerge from mindless physical states. Previously Dennett had offered what he calls a 'synchronic' solution to this problem, considering the relationship between the mind as an 'intentional system' of beliefs and desires and the human body (and more particularly the brain) as a physical organism. Evolution, by contrast, provided a 'diachronic, or historical' answer, by tracing the enormously long series of gradual adaptations which finally gave rise to intentionality.[4] Some discussion of Dennett's philosophy of mind was thus necessary to fill in the intellectual context of his Darwin book.

Secondly, my praise of the book, while justifiable in terms of its philosophical strengths, also involved a certain bending of the stick. In a cultural climate where postmodernism has exercised a pernicious influence, in particular by denying that human thought can genuinely engage with the world, here was a philosopher concerned to apply his analytical skills to articulating and defending one of the most powerful theories ever formulated about that world. It therefore seemed to me important to hold up this kind of work as an example of what philosophers can but too often don't do.

Thirdly, however, none of this implied a general endorsement of Dennett's philosophical position. How could it, when a substantial section of my piece is devoted to criticising him as a mechanical materialist, in particular for taking over Richard Dawkins's ridiculous idea of memes as the equivalents in human culture of genes in living organisms?[5] Joe complains that I don't mention Dennett's alleged empiricism, but there are plenty of other mistaken positions of his—for example, his endorsement in some of his writings of a 'methodological solipsism', which requires us to 'ignore the environment in which the organism resides'—with which I also disagree.[6] Why list all my disagreements with Dennett in an article devoted specifically to his treatment of Darwin?

Minds and computers

John devotes the bulk of his article to a critique of the idea associated with the study of Artificial Intelligence (AI) that, as he puts it, 'a brain…is just a machine that carries out computational processes'.[7] What he says is interesting and, at least in general terms, true. I'm not sure how to the point it is, since I certainly don't think that that the brain, let alone consciousness, is a computer. More interestingly, it's not clear to me that Dennett does.

There are, it seems to me, two basic reasons why minds aren't computers. (For the sake of simplicity, in what follows I don't consistently distinguish between mind and brain.) The first, which John doesn't really discuss, is that human beings are *organisms*. Because of this we have all sorts of needs—for food, shelter, clothing, sex, etc—and capacities—for locomotion, manipulation, articulate speech, and so on—to which there are no real analogies in computers. These needs and capacities underlie and interact with our mental activities. This is important, not simply because we can't understand how humans behave except in the light of these needs and capacities, but because any historical explanation of how human mental life developed can only do so by looking at how this process interacted with the evolution of these needs and capacities in successive species of hominids.

This is, I take it, part of what Trotsky is getting at when he says that 'the psyche could not even have been formed unless it played an autonomous…role in the life of the individual and the species'. In other words, the growing complexity of hominids' brains gave them a selective advantage culminating in the emergence of human society. One of the strengths of the Darwinian strand in Dennett's philosophy of mind is the emphasis it places on the evolutionary process through which human minds developed—although, as I pointed out in my earlier piece, perhaps because of his 'methodological solipsism' he fails to place sufficient emphasis on the role played by labour and language in this history.[8]

The second reason why minds cannot be treated like computers is that, as John argues at some length, brains don't work like computers. But I don't think Dennett thinks so either. John declares that 'Dennett's computer model of mind is one of the primary forms of reductionism operating in psychology today',[9] but the only evidence he cites in support of this assertion is Dennett's declaration in *Consciousness Explained* that 'what you are is the programme that runs on your brain's computer'. This is strong stuff indeed—Dennett himself says he is making a claim in a 'provocative form'—but it needs to be put in the context of his larger account of the mind, something which John fails to do, but which must be attempted here, at least briefly.[10]

In the first place, when reading assertions such as that just cited we have to keep in mind Dennett's overall characterisation of his aim as 'to replace one family of metaphors and images with another' when thinking about the mind.[11] Now a metaphor is a sentence which is literally false but whose assertion illuminates some resemblance or relationship we might not otherwise have noticed.[12] The Earth isn't really shaped like an orange, but when my primary school teacher said that it was, I began to get some sense of its actual shape.

Dennett's 'family of metaphors', including the claim that the self is a computer programme, are directed at a mistaken view of the brain, what he calls 'Cartesian materialism'. The 17th century philosopher Descartes argued that the mind is a *res cogitans*, a thinking thing distinct from the body, from which we view and come to know the world. Cartesian materialism is what we get when we give up this dualistic conception of mind as separate from body, but keep the 'idea of a special centre in the brain' which is the seat of consciousness. Dennett calls this 'the most tenacious bad idea bedevilling our attempts to think about consciousness'. Consciousness is not a show being performed in a 'Cartesian Theatre' somewhere in the brain. He wants to establish that, in fact, *'there's nobody home*. No part of the brain is the thinker that does the thinking or the feeler that does the feeling, and the whole brain appears to be no better candidate for that very special role'.[13]

This leads to Dennett to formulate what he calls 'the Multiple Drafts model of consciousness', according to which 'all varieties of perception—indeed, all varieties of thought or mental activity—are accomplished in the brain, by parallel, multi-track processes of inter-

pretation and elaboration of sensory inputs'. Different parts of the
brain are continually and simultaneously registering information as a
result of our interaction with the world, but:

> ...once a particular 'observation' of some feature has been made, by a spe-
> cialized, localized portion of the brain, the information content thus fixed
> does not have to be sent somewhere else to be rediscriminated by some
> 'master' discriminator. In other words, discrimination does not lead to a **rep-**
> **resentation** of an already discriminated feature for the benefit of the audience
> of the Cartesian Theatre—for there is no Cartesian Theatre... These [spa-
> tially and temporally] distributed content-discriminations yield, over the
> course of time, something **rather like** a narrative stream or sequence, which
> can be thought of as subject to continual editing by many processes distrib-
> uted around in the brain, and continuing indefinitely into the future. This
> stream of contents is only rather like a narrative because of its multiplicity; at
> any point in time there are 'multiple drafts' of narrative fragments at various
> stages of editing in various places in the brain.[14]

I have cited Dennett's description of his model of consciousness at
some length in order to underline one point. The brain depicted here as
an inherently decentred assemblage of simultaneously occurring
processes is very significantly different from any digital computer. The
latter is constructed on principles devised by Alan Turing and Johann
von Neumann. Their work designed a 'virtual machine' involving 'a
serial process (events happening one at a time)' in which 'a finite set of
primitive operations' are repeated over and over again at high speed, so
that 'all the activity of the system has to pass single-file through a narrow
gap.' Dennett comments:

> These fascinating new von Neumann machines...were, in fact, giant elec-
> tronic minds, electronic imitations—severe simplifications—of what William
> James dubbed the stream of consciousness, the meandering sequence of con-
> scious mental contents famously depicted by James Joyce in his novels. The
> architecture of the brain, in contrast, is massively parallel, with millions of
> simultaneously active channels of operation. What we have to understand is
> how a Joycean (or, as I have said, 'von Neumannesque') serial phenomenon
> can come to exist, with all its familiar peculiarities, in the parallel hubbub of
> the brain.[15]

Dennett thus acknowledges that '[t]here is a big difference between a
(standard) computer's serial architecture and the parallel architecture of
the brain'. Yet we undoubtedly *experience* our consciousness as a serial
process, as a stream of consciousness in which one thing follows

another, however randomly. One of Dennett's main concerns is to show how such 'Joycean machines' emerge despite the fact that they are not based in the physical structure of the brain. He argues that they are a product of human cultural evolution in the 150,000 years since our brains reached their current size and complexity:

> In our brains there is a cobbled-together collection of specialist brain-circuits, which, thanks to a family of habits inculcated partly by culture and partly by individual self-exploration, conspire together to produce a more or less orderly, more or less effective, more or less well-designed virtual machine, the **Joycean machine**. By yoking these independently evolved specialist organs together in common cause, and thereby giving their union vastly enhanced powers, this virtual machine, this software of the brain, performed a sort of internal political miracle: it creates a **virtual capture** of the crew, without elevating any of them to long-term dictatorial power.[16]

Now whatever one may think of this theory of consciousness, it is not in any straightforward way reductionist. Dennett's use of a whole array of computer-generated metaphors for the mind is intended in part, as he says, to provoke, to challenge the residual idealist conception of the mind as 'a ghost in the machine', a mysterious spiritual essence lurking somewhere behind the physical circuits in the brain. It is also because, despite the fact that there are, as he says, 'important—and often overlooked—**dis**analogies' between minds and computers, comparing them can help to explain the phenomenon of consciousness.[17]

Dennett's theory has been subjected to searching criticism by other philosophers.[18] But even if many of these criticisms are valid, it doesn't seem to me that his enterprise is inherently a disreputable one. It will not do, as John does, simply to reaffirm the differences between human beings and, on the one hand, other animals, and, on the other hand, computers. Real though these differences are, humans are, after all, physical organisms, and any materialist account of the human mind is going to have to come up with some way of relating mental and physical states. If not Dennett's way, then what? I'm sure that there are other, perhaps more fruitful ways, but John doesn't acknowledge the existence of the problem.

Moreover he implies that *any* comparison between minds and computers is necessarily a case of alienation. This smacks of the attitude of those philosophers like John Seatle and Colin McGinn whom Dennett denounces as 'mysterians' because they treat the mind as something too sublime and ineffable to be compared with anything as vulgar as a mere machine. Materialism necessarily requires us to see mind as part of nature, including what Hegel calls human-made 'second nature'.

Comparisons between minds and computers should be judged on their merits and not ruled out *a priori*.

Joe shows more awareness of the issue when he takes Dennett to task for having what he calls an empiricist conception of intentionality. In other words, Dennett argues that we should treat something as an 'intentional system', ascribing to it beliefs and desires, when this proves to be the best way of predicting how it will behave. Doing so involves making no judgement about what real properties the intentional system has that are responsible for it behaving in a way that is best treated as the outcome of beliefs and desires.[19]

Undoubtedly Dennett does advance such a conception of intentionality, which I would prefer to call pragmatist rather than empiricist, though I won't quibble about words. Dennett himself describes this approach as 'Interpretivism' and defends it on philosophical grounds too complex to go into here.[20] All the same, Joe is right: treating intentionality as a predictive device does not amount to an explanation of mental life, since that would require identifying the real properties that, for example, human beings have which account for our holding beliefs and desires and acting on them. But this merely reinforces the point I made above. Any such explanation of human mental activities is going to have to come up with some story of how they hook up with the body in general and the brain in particular. Dennett's merit is to have come up with one such story which avoids the more obvious forms of reductionism; for example, the idea that there is a direct correlation between individual events, physical states and individual mental events.[21]

Joes's own attempt at an explanation, even taking constraints of space into account, doesn't even begin to address the problem:

> *To put it crudely, what makes our thoughts of a cat **about** a cat (rather than being a purely private, internal, affair)? The simple answer is that our thoughts can cause our bodies to reach out and grab a cat, and so bring our contents into contact with their contents through our actions.*[22]

But this won't do at all. Dennett calls intentionality 'the "aboutness" that can relate one thing to another'.[23] In other words, our beliefs and desires pick out items in the world in order to ascribe to them properties which we either hold they have or wish they had. The ability of our thoughts to refer to objects in this way is undoubtedly bound up with our causal interactions with the world.[24] But they cannot be reduced to these interactions. Dogs causally interact with cats, but this doesn't mean that Fido when chasing Moggy consciously entertains any of the following thoughts: 'I like chasing cats', 'Moggy is a cat', 'I want to kill Moggy', or even, 'Here is Moggy'. Whatever proto-beliefs and desires we must attribute to Fido in order to explain his behaviour as what Dennett might call a 'semi-intentional system', they do not form an articulated system of thoughts used to refer to and make assertions about different parts of the world.[25] More than anything else, it is the fact that human thought and language are both holist—in other words, our various beliefs and desires interconnect with each other to form a whole—and referential—these beliefs and desires point beyond themselves to the world—that makes it so difficult satisfactorily to identify the physical basis of our mental life. Only a materialism that is fully aware of this difficulty can hope to overcome it.

Evolution, contingency, and chance

Though Joe here lapses into a sort of crude materialism, the general drift of his remarks on evolution is in a somewhat idealist direction. In effect, he accuses me of being too sympathetic to the orthodox Darwinian conception of evolution defended by Dennett. Before I deal directly with what he has to say, it may be helpful to set out some of the main issues that divide orthodox Darwinians such as Dennett and the biologists Richard Dawkins and John Maynard Smith from what one might call their 'left Darwinian' critics such as Stephen Jay Gould, Richard Levins, Richard Lewontin, and Stephen Rose:

The unit of selection
Darwin argued that natural selection is the main force responsible for the emergence of new species: variations which enhance an organism's 'differential fitness'—its ability to survive and reproduce relative to other organisms in the same environment—and which can be passed on to its offspring will, other things being equal, lead to its descendants making up a larger proportion of future generations. But what exactly is it that is selected in this process? Is it, as Darwin thought, the individual organism? Is it, as many naturalists have believed, a larger group of organisms—the population or even the species? Or is it, as Dawkins argued in *The Selfish Gene*, the individual gene?[26]

Adaptation
Adaptation is a key Darwinian concept. Advantageous variations make organisms better adapted to their environment: the adaptation allows the organism either to cope better with an environment that has remained unchanged, or to respond to changes in the environment. But Gould and Lewontin have attacked what they call orthodox Darwinian 'adaptationism', which tries to explain every trait of an organism as an adaptation and to adopt a 'Panglossian' view of evolution in which which the entire

array of life is constantly tending towards a state of 'optimal' adaptation to the world around it (in Voltaire's novel *Candide* Dr Pangloss is constantly explaining away everything, good or bad, as a consequence of the fact that 'all is for the best in this best of all possible worlds').[27]

Punctuated equilibrium
Darwin wrote:

> *I believe that natural selection will always act very slowly, often only at long intervals of time, and generally on a very few inhabitants of the same region at the same time. I further believe that this very slow, intermittent action of natural selection accords very well with what geology tells us of the rate and manner at which the inhabitants of this world have changed.*[28]

This conception of natural selection as an extremely slow process of gradual change is defended by contemporary orthodox Darwinians. Thus Dawkins in what is probably his best book, *The Blind Watchmaker*, provides very effective arguments in support of Darwin's thesis that all the complexity of the living world, apparent evidence of design, can be explained as a consequence of the 'very slow, intermittent action of natural selection'.

One difficulty with this approach is that, *pace* Darwin, the fossil record has never supported his conception of evolution as a series of continual, small scale changes, since markedly new species tend to appear very abruptly. Darwin devoted much effort to explaining away what he acknowledged to be the problem posed by this *'absence or rarity of transitional varieties'*.[29] But Gould and his fellow palaeontologist Nils Eldredge have suggested that we should instead take the fossil record at face value. For them evolution is a process of 'punctuated equilibrium', in which long periods of stasis, where little or no adaptation occurs, is interrupted by relatively concentrated bursts of qualitative change. To explain this pattern, they further argue, it is necessary to posit forms of group selection, thus coming into conflict with more orthodox conceptions of the selection of genes or individual organisms.[30]

Contingency
Gould goes even further in more recent writings, notably his book *Wonderful Life* (1989). He argues that the actual path taken by evolution must not be seen as some sort of necessary pattern. He insists instead on 'the controlling power of contingency in setting the pattern of life's history and current composition'.[31] The great late Cretaceous extinction 65 million years ago provides an example familiar to every school child. Probably the most popular explanation of this extinction, in which most

of the dinosaurs died, is that it was caused by the environmental disruption that followed a large comet hitting the Earth.[32] Without this collision, which could hardly be predicted on the basis of the properties of living organisms alone, the mammals might still be small rat-like creatures furtively scurrying around at the dinosaurs' feet. So the development of the mammals, culminating, as triumphalist presentations of evolution tend to, in the emergence of *Homo sapiens sapiens*, turns out to be the product of what is, from the perspective of the life-sciences, an accident.

It is in this sense that Gould argues that natural history is permeated by 'contingency':

> We call a historical event...contingent when it occurs as a chancy result of a long string of unpredictable antecedents, rather than as a necessary outcome of nature's laws. Such contingent events often depend upon choices from a distant past that seemed tiny and trivial at the time. Minor perturbations early in the game can nudge a process into a new pathway, with cascading consequences that produce an outcome vastly different from any alternative.[33]

These are large and complex issues, and it may seem a bit of a cheek for a non-biologist to express definite opinions on some of them, but here goes anyway.[34] It seems to me that on the first and second points the left-Darwinians are right. The effect of their arguments is to undermine the image of evolution promoted by Dawkins and other orthodox Darwinians as an interaction between individual genes and their environment.

On the one hand, the relationship between gene and phenotype (the actual organism) posited by Dawkins's 'genic selectionism' depends on what the philosopher Elliott Sober calls 'beanbag genetics', where 'each gene would produce a single phenotypic characteristic of selective importance. Possessing a gene would then be a positive causal factor for possessing the phenotype in question'. But beanbag genetics is undermined by two phenomena: first, *pleiotropy,* where the same gene may have more than one phenotypic effect, and not all these effects confer selective advantages; secondly, *polygenic effects,* 'in which', as Sober puts it, 'a given phenotype is the result of an interaction among an ensemble of genes'.[35] So genic selectionism fails because it posits an atomistic relationship between gene and pheontype.

On the other hand, Levins and Lewontin challenge the idea which underlies the concept of adaptation, of the organism fitting a pre-existing environment. In the first place, organisms interact with and change their environment: Darwin in his last book celebrated the role of the humble earthworm in creating the soil itself. Secondly, however, the features of the environment relevant to a given organism will depend on the nature of the organism itself. So there is an important sense in which the environment cannot be characterised independently of the organism itself; consequently, adaptation cannot be seen simply as a matter of organisms responding to problems posed by an environment independent of them. Finally, an important role is played by '*developmental noise*, the random events at a cellular and molecular level that influence cell maturation and division and that especially may result in small differences in the time when critical divisions occur'. Therefore, 'The consequences of the interaction of gene, environment, and developmental noise is a many-to-many relationship between gene and organism. The same genotype gives rise to many different organisms, and the same organism can correspond to many different genotypes.'[36]

Now Joe argues that this 'constructionist' (as Lewontin describes it) conception of the relationship between organism and environment supports Gould's stress on contingency: 'once organisms define their own conditions, then the variability in the initial population can quickly lead to very divergent histories'.[37] And Lewontin himself writes:

At every moment in the life history of an organism there is contingency of development such that the next step is dependent on the current state of the organism and the environmental signals that are impinging on it. Simply, the organism is a unique result of both its genes and the temporal sequence of environments through which it has passed, and there is no way of knowing in advance, from the DNA sequence, what the organism will look like, except in general terms.[38]

A number of points are worth making here. In the first place, it's necessary to treat the claim that 'organisms define their own conditions' with some care. To say, as Levins and Lewontin do, that '[o]rganisms determine what aspects of their environment are relevant and which environmental variations can be lumped or ignored,' is not to say that they in general *control* their environment.[39] Their different, genetically based relationships to their environments must explain why mammals survived, and dinosaurs mostly perished in the late Cretaceous extinction, but neither *caused* the cometary collison apparently responsible for this biological upheaval. The idea of organisms defining their environment, while a useful corrective to the orthodox Darwinian conception of adaptation, can, unless used carefully, have idealist connotations.

Secondly, to say that the actual path of development taken by an organism cannot be predicted from its DNA is not to say that it cannot be explained. It is possible, in principle, to reconstruct the way in which the organism's genes, 'the temporal sequence of the environments through which it has passed', and 'developmental noise' interacted to produce the actual course it followed. This may be a retrospective exercise, but then the study of living organisms, like that of human societies, neces sarily requires the historical reconstruction of processes that unfolded in the past.

Thirdly, these historical reconstructions undoubtedly involve an element of contingency in the sense that there are a number—perhaps a very large number—of developmental paths in principle consistent with the same genotype. It is precisely for this reason that an organism's actual development can be the subject of a historical narrative which seeks to capture the particularities which led it along the path it took. In that sense Gould's stress on the importance of natural *history* in his recent writings is entirely correct and praiseworthy.[40]

Nevertheless, these possible paths are subject to a number of constraints. One is provided by the laws of inorganic nature: organic evolution must respect such physical realities as gravitation and the conservation of energy (though, as Lewontin, points out, the effect of these forces is filtered through the genetic structure of the organisms concerned: gravity is a burden for large mammals such as us but not for bacteria).[41] Another is provided by the laws of genetics and of biological structure: whatever the variations in the environments that I encounter, I am never going to sprout wings and fly, or turn into a typewriter. Then there is the phenomenon of 'convergent evolution', in Gould's words, 'the repeated development of similar adaptations in different lineages', or what Dennett calls 'forced (or good) moves'. The same problem may pose itself to a wide variety of organisms, nudging them towards the same solution: the eye is a good example, since it has evolved independently on a number of different occasions.[42]

Whatever contingency there is in natural history occurs within the framework of these, and no doubt other constraints. Evolution is thus neither random nor arbitrary, even if it is unpredictable. Maybe Gould would accept all the above provisos to his thesis about historical contingency. Indeed, occasionally he makes analogous points, asserting for example, 'Invariant laws of nature impact the general forms and functions of organisms; they set the channels in which organic designs must evolve.' But, characteristically, he then takes away much of what he has apparently conceded: 'When we set our focus upon the level of detail that regulates most common questions about the history of life, contingency dominates and the predictability of general form recedes to an irrelevant background'.[43]

In advancing this thesis Gould seems to be bending the stick against vulgar Darwinian identifications of the concept of evolution with 'some notion of progress, usually inherent and predictable, and leading to a human pinnacle'. If so, he nevertheless does at times bend the stick to the point of breaking, as when he identifies himself with:

...the most philosophically radical concept arising from our modern study of life's early multicellular history—the notion that most losses occurred by the luck of the draw rather than by the predictable superiority of a few founding lineages, and that any particular lineage still alive today (including our own) owes its existence to the contingency of good fortune.[44]

Does Joe agree with this? Is evolution simply a lottery in which survival or extinction is determined by 'the luck of the draw'? To answer the latter question in the affirmative is to come dangerously close to abandoning the claim—central to Darwin's theory of natural selection—of being able to explain the evolution of organisms. Gould is a brilliant populariser of that theory's successes, and its vigilant defender against the inroads of 'creation science', so it is surprising to see him pull the rug from under himself and the rest of the Darwinian camp. The reason is, I have suggested, a reaction to the kind of triumphalism characteristic of vulgarisations of evolutionary theory. But in seeking to differentiate himself from this he does not seem to notice that he is thrusting himself into the arms of other foes—not just the creationists who eagerly seek to exploit any disagreement among evolutionary biologists, but also post-modernists happy to the use the writings of a leading scientific populariser to prove that natural as well as human history is nothing but the play of 'contingency'.[45]

Conclusion

This brings me to a more general point on which I shall conclude. Biological reductionism—as represented, for example, by Dawkins's genic selectionism—is not merely a theoretical error but a ideological threat. It serves to justify a whole series of practical projects which seek to control or alter people's behaviour or to legitimise their oppression on the basis of their genes—the idea that IQ tests reflect inherent differences in intelligence, the Human Genome Project, and so on.[46] The left Darwinians have provided a brilliant critique of such nostrums: Gould's *The Mismeasure of Man* in particular stands out as a devastating historical and scientific demolition of the whole wretched business of IQ testing.

But we should not be led, either out of gratitude to the left Darwinians or because of the real intellectual substance of their work, into one of two errors. One is to assume that orthodox Darwinians like Dennett and Dawkins are always wrong. As John has himself pointed out, Dawkins, despite his genic selectionism, is a superb expositor of the theory of natural selection, who has defended it very effectively against the mystifications of creationism.[47] Indeed, like Dennett, he is something of an old fashioned Victorian mechanical materialist, who overstates the importance of a purely intellectual struggle against Christianity, astrology, and other superstitions, as opposed to Marxism's effort to identify and address their social causes.

The second and related error is to adopt an uncritical attitude towards the left Darwinians. Important, indeed simply brilliant as their work often is, they are liable for a variety of reasons—overreaction to biological reductionism and vulgar Darwinism, their social position as academics relatively isolated from working class organisation and struggle, in some cases conceptions of 'radical science' of Maoist derivation—to react to the mechanical materialism of which Dennett and Dawkins are often guilty by lapsing into various forms of idealism. Gould's tendency to reduce natural history to contingency is a case in point.

Though I am grateful to John and Joe for the opportunity their articles have given me to discuss these issues, I think that, in their reaction to my original review of Dennett's book, they show a certain tendency towards this kind of left Darwinian idealism. We have much to learn from Gould, Lewontin, Rose et al, and will often find ourselves fighting alongside them, but we should not therefore abandon our critical faculties or refuse to learn from other currents in evolutionary theory.

Notes

1   L Trotsky, *Philosophical Notebooks* (New York, 1986), p106.
2   Ibid, p107.
3   A Callinicos, 'Darwin, Materialism and Evolution', *International Socialism* 2.71 (1996); J Parrington, 'Computers and Consciousness', and J Faith, 'Dennett, Materialism, and Empiricism', both in *International Socialism* 2.73 (1996).
4   See especially D C Dennett, *Darwin's Dangerous Idea* (London, 1995), pp205-206.
5   A Callinicos, op cit, pp106-112.
6   D C Dennett, 'Beyond Belief', in A Woodfield (ed), *Thought and Object* (Oxford, 1982), p25.
7   J Parrington, op cit, p55.
8   See C Harman, 'Engels and the Origins of Human Society', *International Socialism* 2.65 (1995), pp84-104.
9   J Parrington, op cit, p55.
10   D C Dennett, *Consciousness Explained* (London, 1993), p430.
11   Ibid, p455.
12   See D Davidson, 'What Metaphors Mean', *Inquiries into Truth and Interpretation* (Oxford, 1984).
13   D C Dennett, op cit, pp29, 108.
14   Ibid, pp111, 113.
15   Ibid, pp212, 214. 'A virtual machine is what you get when you impose a particular pattern of rules...on all that plasticity'—ie that possessed in different ways by both computers and brains: ibid, p211.
16   Ibid, pp215, 228. See generally ibid, chs 7 and 8.

17   Ibid, p219. See A Callinicos, op cit, pp101-102, for a brief account of the role
      played by metaphors derived from AI in Dennett's earlier work in the philosophy
      of mind.
18   See Dahlbom (ed), *Dennett and his Critics* (Oxford, 1993).
19   J Faith, op cit, pp67-69; compare, eg, D C Dennett, *Brainstorms* (Brighton, 1981),
      especially ch 1.
20   See especially J Fodor and E Lepore, 'Is Intentional Ascription Intrinsically
      Normative?', R Rorty, 'Holism, Intrinsicality, and the Ambition of Transcendence',
      and D C Dennett, 'Back to the Drawing Board', all in Dahlbom, op cit.
21   For a classic critique of this kind of physicalism, see D Davidson, *Essays on
      Actions and Events* (Oxford, 1980), essays 11-13.
22   J Faith, op cit, p68.
23   D C Dennett, *Darwin's Dangerous Idea*, op cit, p205.
24   G Evans, *The Varieties of Reference* (Oxford, 1982).
25   Dennett discusses the whole issue of animal consciousness in *Kinds of Minds*
      (London, 1996).
26   E Sober, *The Nature of Selection* (Chicago, 1993), Part II.
27   S J Gould and R C Lewontin, 'The Spandrels of San Marco', *Proceedings of the
      Royal Society* B205 (1979).
28   C Darwin, *The Origin of Species by Means of Natural Selection* (Harmondsworth,
      1968), p153.
29   Ibid, p206.
30   See N Eldredge, *Reinventing Darwin* (London, 1996).
31   S J Gould, *Wonderful Life* (London, 1991), p289.
32   See S J Gould, 'The Belt of an Asteroid', in *Hen's Teeth and Horses' Toes*
      (Harmondsworth, 1984), and M Davies, 'Cosmic Dancers on Earth's Stage?', *New
      Left Review* 217 (1996), especially p55ff.
33   S J Gould, *Bully for Brontosaurus* (Harmondsworth, 1992), p69; see also S J
      Gould, *Wonderful Life*, op cit, pp277-291.
34   I say nothing here about the question of punctuated equilibrium because I simply
      lack the competence to judge whether Gould and Eldgredge or their orthodox
      Darwinian opponents are right. It is not in any case quite so obvious how much
      hangs on which side is right here as it is with respect to the other issues. The idea
      of punctuated equilibrium is an attractive one for Marxists since it seems to be an
      instance of the dialectical law of transformation of quantity into quality, but that is
      not, on its own, sufficient reason for accepting it.
35   E Sober, op cit, pp312-313. See also S J Gould, 'Caring Groups and Selfish
      Genes', in *The Panda's Thumb* (Harmondsworth, 1983).
36   R Levins and R C Lewontin, *The Dialectical Biologist* (Cambridge MA, 1985),
      pp93-94. See also ibid, part I, and R C Lewontin, 'Genes, Environments, and
      Organisms', in R B Silvers (ed), *Hidden Histories of Science* (London, 1997).
37   J Faith, op cit, p70. Joe also says that I present 'a one-sided picture of natural
      selection [as] being primarily about competition for resources'. This is, I think, a
      strained reading of my exposition of Darwin's theory (Callinicos, op cit, pp103-
      104, and see also pp113-114 n15). Darwin himself stressed, 'I use the Struggle for
      Existence in a large and metaphorical sense', and that competition may be 'one
      individual with another of the same species, or with the individuals of distinct
      species, *or with the physical conditions of life*' (C Darwin, op cit, pp116-117;
      emphasis added). So 'the Struggle for Existence' may pit an organism against its
      environment rather than against other organisms.
38   C R Lewontin, 'Genes, Environments, and Organisms', op cit, p124.
39   R Levins and C R Lewontin, op cit, p55.

40   See, for example, S J Gould, *Wonderful Life*, op cit, pp277-291, and 'George Canning's Left Buttock and the Evolution of Species', in *Bully for Brontosaurus*, op cit.

41   C R Lewontin, 'Genes, Environments, and Organisms', op cit, pp136-137.

42   S J Gould, *The Panda's Thumb*, op cit, p35; see also D C Dennett, *Darwin's Dangerous Idea*, op cit, pp128ff.

43   S J Gould, *Wonderful Life*, op cit, pp289, 290.

44   S J Gould, 'Ladders and Cones', in R B Silvers (ed), op cit, *Hidden Histories of Science*, pp42-43, 67.

45   Thus see Gould's correspondence with ex-president Jimmy Carter where the latter seizes on his claim in *Wonderful Life* that '*Homo sapiens*...is a wildly improbable evolutionary event' (p291) to argue for divine creation: S J Gould, 'In a Jumbled Drawer', in *Bully for Brontosaurus*, op cit. Gould's highly technical answer is, to say the least, unconvincing.

46   See R C Lewontin, *The Doctrine of DNA* (London, 1993).

47   J Parrington, 'No Mere Gene Programme', *Socialist Worker*, 7 September 1996.

In perspective: Noam Chomsky

ANTHONY ARNOVE

No writer in the second half of the 20th century has done as much to document and expose the crimes of US imperialism as Noam Chomsky. A
linguist who has taught for the last 40 years at the Massachusetts
Institute of Technology, and who has made tremendous advances in the
understanding of human language, Chomsky has accumulated since the
early 1960s an unequalled body of detailed investigations of US foreign
policy, its impact on domestic politics, and the apologetics of intellectuals who defend the crimes committed in the name of 'human rights'
and 'support for democracy'.

From his early essays in the liberal intellectual journal *The New York
Review of Books* to his most recent books, *Powers and Prospects* (1996)
and *World Orders Old and New* (second edition, 1996), Chomsky has
produced a singular body of political criticism. *American Power and the
New Mandarins* (1969), his first published collection of political writing
(dedicated 'To the brave young men who refuse to serve in a criminal
war'), contains essays that still stand out for their insight and biting
sarcasm three decades later. 'It is easy to be carried away by the sheer
horror of what the daily press reveals [about the American war in
Vietnam] and to lose sight of the fact that this is merely the brutal exte-
rior of a deeper crime, of commitment to a social order that guarantees
endless suffering and humiliation and denial of elementary human
rights', Chomsky wrote in this first collection, setting himself apart from
the vast majority of the war's critics who saw it as a 'tragic mistake',

rather than as an example of American imperialism.[1]

Since 1969 Chomsky has produced a series of books on US foreign policy in Asia, Latin America and the Middle East. Chomsky's well documented *Fateful Triangle* remains an indispensable study of the history of Israeli state terrorism and the extensive US government support for 'an Israeli Sparta as a strategic asset'; the book's rigorous dismantling of the official Zionist version of the Arab-Israeli conflict and its outspoken support for Palestinian self determination still stand out.[2]

Chomsky has also made an important contribution to the international effort to raise awareness of the struggle to free East Timor, a former Portuguese colony that was invaded in 1975 by Indonesia and then annexed with full support from the United States government, leading to the deaths of over 200,000 Timorese. He has devoted endless hours of writing, lecturing, and patient one-on-one conversation to bring attention to these events and to US support of state terrorism in Latin America, Israeli aggression in the West Bank, Gaza and Lebanon, and the role of the establishment media in keeping such unpleasant details well hidden.

More recently Chomsky has taken an active stance against the Gulf War and the 1993-95 Oslo Accords, which he pointed out represented an overwhelming 'rejectionist victory' for Israel and the United States, though many leading leftists supported the Gulf intervention and celebrated the PLO-Israeli agreement.[3] Chomsky's writings on the Oslo document are in the best tradition of his work, outlining the exact scope and gravity of the Palestinian defeat and the PLO's responsibility for betraying the struggle for Palestinian liberation.

It is no exaggeration, as the *New York Times Review of Books* argued in 1979, that, 'judged in terms of the power, range, novelty and influence of his thought, Noam Chomsky is arguably the most important intellectual alive today'.[4]

Chomsky has developed a damning political critique of contemporary capitalism and has done much materially to support numerous organisations involved in efforts for social change, however, his comments on strategies for transforming society are far less compelling and raise important difficulties. To see why, it is necessary to examine Chomsky's commitment to anarchism (or, as he has also called it, 'libertarian socialism'), his critique of Bolshevism, the Russian Revolution and the role of Lenin and Trotsky in it, and his anti-Marxism.

Chomsky's background

To understand Noam Chomsky's ideas, we have to look in part at his personal and intellectual history and the political roots of his anarchism. Chomsky was born in Philadelphia on 7 December 1928 and raised in a

Jewish-Zionist cultural tradition, among Eastern European immigrants. His father, William Chomsky, fled from Russia in 1913 to escape conscription into the Tsarist army. His mother, Elsie Simonofsky, left Lithuania when she was one year old.

Chomsky grew up during the Depression and the rise of the fascist threat internationally. As he later recalled, 'Some of my earliest memories, which are very vivid, are of people selling rags at our door, of violent police strikebreaking, and other Depression scenes'.[5] 'In the 1930s it was pretty clear that the Nazis were a very ominous and dangerous force that was like a dark cloud over everything throughout my whole childhood'.[6] After a 1995 meeting in which he helped raise money for locked out paper workers, Chomsky recalled:

> *The other night in the meeting on Decatur they showed a video on police violence. I remember that very well from 1934-1935, with much worse scenes of police attacking. I remember I was with my mother on a trolley car. I must have been five years old. There was a textile strike. Women workers were picketing. We just passed by and saw a very violent police attack on women strikers.*[7]

> *I can't claim that I understood what was happening, but I sort of got the general idea. What I didn't understand was explained to me... My family had plenty of unemployed workers and union activists and political activists and so on. So you knew what a picket line was and what it meant for the forces of the employers to come in there swinging clubs and breaking it up.*[8]

Chomsky grew up around working class people, ideas and organisation, and was imbued at an early age with a sense of class solidarity and struggle.

While his parents were 'normal Roosevelt Democrats', he had aunts and uncles who were garment workers in the ILGWU, Communists, Trotskyists and anarchists. As a child, Chomsky was influenced by the radical Jewish intellectual culture in New York City. He regularly visited the Jewish anarchist newspapers and bookstores on Fourth Avenue. According to Chomsky, this was a 'working class culture with working class values, solidarity, socialist values... Within that it varied from Communist Party to radical semi-anarchist critique of Bolshevism. That whole range was there'.[9]

Among this range of ideas though, Chomsky was particularly influenced by his aunt's husband, a fourth grade dropout who ran a news stand on the Upper West Side of New York on 72nd Street and Broadway. 'First he was a follower of Trotsky, then an anti-Trotskyite', according to Chomsky.[10] It was clearly the anti-Trotskyist, anarchist critique of Bolshevism that made the most lasting impression on Chomsky's political thinking.

At a very young age Chomsky understood that the Communist Party under Stalin was intervening decisively against the interests of the Spanish working class and had acted to crush the workers' revolution that had been initiated in the midst of the Spanish Civil War (1936-39). Chomsky's first political article—on the fall of Barcelona to the fascists—was written when he was only ten years old. The CP's counter-revolution against the Spanish workers, who had started to collectivise land and seize control of factories in some areas, and establish militias without traditional ranks in their battle against the fascists and Franco, had a lasting impact on him.[11] Chomsky saw Stalinism as a natural outgrowth of the theory and practice of Lenin, Trotsky, and the Bolshevik Party—the view that Chomsky still holds today.[12] Chomsky later wrote that the CP's suppression of the Spanish Revolution demonstrates 'the extent to which Bolshevism and Western liberalism have been united in their opposition to popular revolution'.[13]

The impact of this early commitment to anarchism cannot be over-emphasised. It has decisively shaped Chomsky's political and intellectual career. By the age of 13 Chomsky identified with 'the anti-Bolshevik left' and had come to feel that he was isolated in his revolutionary ideals. 'I was always on the side of the losers—the Spanish anarchists, for example', he later commented.[14] '[E]ver since I had any political awareness, I've felt either alone or part of a tiny minority'.[15] Chomsky might be just another Jewish Philadelphia radical or anarchist though, were it not for his turn to the study of language in the 1940s.

Chomsky's contribution to linguistics

After having almost dropped out of the University of Pennsylvania, where he had enrolled as an undergraduate when he was 16, Chomsky found intellectual and political stimulation from the Russian linguist, Professor Zelig Harris. Influenced by his parents, both of whom taught Hebrew, Chomsky gravitated toward the unusual intellectual milieu around Harris. Harris, active in the Zionist Avukah organisation, taught seminars on linguistics that involved philosophical debates, reading and independent research outside the standard constraints of the university structure.

Chomsky began graduate work with Harris, and in 1951 joined Harvard's Society of Fellows, where he continued his research into linguistics. By 1953 Chomsky had broken 'almost entirely from the field as it existed',[16] and was soon publishing path-breaking work, drawing on the 17th century linguistics of the Port-Royal school and the French philosopher René Descartes, and the later work of the Prussian philosopher William von Humboldt, on the 'creative aspect of language use'.[17] Though Chomsky would at times downplay or deny the connection, his political and linguistic work have both built on the idealist philosophical tradition that he has traced back from anarchism through 'classical liberalism' to the Enlightenment and the early rationalists of the 17th century.[18]

In a critical advance over the then dominant understanding of linguistics, Chomsky challenged the behaviourist orthodoxy of B F Skinner, whose views on language he dismantled in an important 1959 critique. As one commentary explains:

> *In the 1950s the social sciences were dominated by behaviourism, the school of thought popularised by John Watson and B F Skinner... Behaviour was explained by a few laws of stimulus-response learning that could be studied with rats pressing bars and dogs salivating to tones. But Chomsky called attention to two fundamental facts about language. First, virtually every sentence that a person utters or understands is a brand-new combination of words, appearing for the first time in the history of the universe. Therefore a language cannot be a repertoire of responses; the brain must contain a recipe or program that can build an unlimited set of sentences out of a finite list of words... The second fundamental fact is that children develop these complex grammars rapidly and without formal instruction and grow up to give consistent interpretations to novel sentence constructions that they have never before encountered. Therefore, he argued, children must innately be equipped with a plan common to the grammars of all languages, a Universal Grammar.*[19]

That is, as Chomsky has written more recently, 'there is a component of the human mind/brain dedicated to language—the language faculty'.[20] According to Chomsky, the 'language faculty' includes a generative system that can produce an infinite array of sentences from finite means. Children don't learn language by imitation, but develop the creative capacity to use language from their infancy at a tremendously fast pace, as the stimulus of their environment 'sets' the parameters of their language. Chomsky argues therefore that standard divisions between languages (whether common sense distinctions between English and French or reactionary ones, say between 'proper English' and 'dialect English') reflect nothing more than superficial or political distinctions within a single, universal and highly complex human language. 'What we call "English", "French", "Spanish",' Chomsky argues, 'reflect the Norman Conquest, proximity to Germanic areas, a Basque substratum, and other factors that cannot seriously be regarded as properties of the language faculty'.[21]

From the early circulation of his linguistic reflections among specialists, Chomsky's views caused considerable controversy and became the subject of intense debates in linguistics, as well as philosophy and the social sciences. Particularly controversial was Chomsky's claim in *Aspects of the Theory of Syntax* that 'linguistic theory is concerned primarily with an ideal speaker-listener, in a completely homogenous speech-community, who knows its language perfectly and is unaffected by such grammatically irrelevant conditions as memory limitations, distractions, shifts of attention and interest, and errors (random or characteristic) in applying his knowledge of the language in actual performance', not to mention by the material, social conditions of the speaker's situation.[22]

What puzzled mainstream commentators far more than his often obscure writings on syntax and semantics, though, was the fact that Chomsky, who joined the faculty of MIT in 1955 at the age of 26 and was beginning to receive tremendous recognition for his linguistic work, was speaking out publicly and participating in direct action against the Vietnam War.

Chomsky's early activism

Though he read political literature and maintained his interest in radical politics in the 1950s, Chomsky spent the bulk of the decade on linguistic work. This changed, however, in the early 1960s, when the United States began its massive onslaught against Southern Vietnam, and Chomsky became active in the anti-war movement. Chomsky participated in one of the first public protests against the war in Boston in October 1965, at which protesters were outnumbered by counter-demonstrators and police. Chomsky helped found the anti-war group Resist in 1966, which organised support for draft resistance, and was arrested for civil disobedience in October 1967 during a Washington, DC, anti-war protest. Resist made connections with some members of the Black Panthers, including Fred Hampton. After Hampton's murder by the FBI and the Chicago police, Chomsky attended his funeral.[23]

Although active in the movement against the war and in the broad New Left, Chomsky held a relatively narrow conception of acceptable forms of protest. He argued at the time that many of the student rebellions were 'largely misguided' for targeting the officials in charge of the universities, criticising student radicals at Berkeley in 1966, at Columbia during the student strike in 1968, and later at MIT.[24] 'I paid virtually no attention to what was going on in Paris [in Spring 1968] as you can see from what I wrote—rightly,' Chomsky recently explained.[25]

Though he helped found Resist, Chomsky dropped out of the day to day activity of the organisation to focus on writing and lecturing, beginning 'a division of labour' between his research and writing and the efforts of activists that has characterised his work since.[26]

Chomsky began to make a wider political mark when he started writing long, detailed essays denouncing the war and the role of mainstream intellectuals who supported it for the *New York Review of Books* and then for left journals such as *Liberation, Ramparts, New Politics,* and *Socialist Revolution* (later *Socialist Review*). These essays brilliantly documented and condemned the actions of the US government in Indochina and connected the war effort to the history of US imperialism more generally. Chomsky became one of the most important and respected critics of the US war effort, earning a place on President Nixon's infamous 'enemies list'. From this point on, he was the subject of intense vilification by various apologists of the system, much as he would later be subjected to repeated attacks for his critical writings on Israel.

In these early essays we see Chomsky developing the basic themes of his best work: rigorously detailed analyses of US planning documents, declassified records, official statements, and hard-to-find sources; merciless critique of liberals, establishment intellectuals, and media commentators who provided a cover for US imperialism; and an analysis which showed that the war in Vietnam was not the result of 'mistakes', 'honest misunderstanding', 'attempts to do good gone awry'—or of bad or incompetent officials who could be replaced by better ones. Rather, the war against Indochina was a product of systematic, deeply rooted features of the capitalist state.

Chomsky's method: 'What is to be done?'

The question of Chomsky's method has been the subject of much debate. Though immensely thought provoking, Chomsky's densely textured political writings suffer from two weaknesses: the lack of a clear theoretical framework and a lack of concreteness about strategies for resistance. As Milan Rai remarks in a recent, highly sympathetic study of Chomsky's political ideas, 'It can sometimes seem as if Chomsky is doing little more than knitting together a mass of fascinating but unrelated insights and facts about US policy' and that—partly as a result—'readers of Chomsky's political writings can be forgiven for feeling that the dominant message of his work is not that "there is a great deal that can be done".'[27]

That is, despite his anti-capitalism, Chomsky offers little practical advice on how to struggle most effectively to bring about the kind of socialist society he would like to see. Though he argues that, whatever one chooses to do politically, it is only effective through organised and collective struggle, Chomsky sets himself apart from socialist organisation and the revolutionary Marxist tradition.

To understand why Chomsky is so reluctant to offer this kind of political lead, we have to return to his anarchism, because one of its features is a hesitancy to argue for specific priorities for political activism. A radio exchange with Chomsky illustrates this problem:

> **Radio listener**: I'm afraid there may be a saturation point of despair just from knowing the heaviness of the truth that you impart. I'd like to strongly lobby you to begin devoting maybe 10 percent or 15 percent of your appearances or books or articles towards tangible, detailed things that people can do to try to change the world. I've heard a few occasions where someone asks you that question and your response is, Organise. Just do it.

> **Chomsky**: I try to keep it in the back of my mind and think about it, but I'm afraid that the answer is always the same...[I]f you join with other people, you can make changes. Millions of things are possible, depending on where you want to put your efforts.[28]

Or, as Chomsky said in two recent interviews:

> The question that comes up over and over again, and I don't really have an answer still, (really, I don't know any other people who have answers to them), is, It's terrible, awful, getting worse. What do we do? Tell me the answer. The trouble is, there has not in history ever been any answer other than, Get to work on it.
>
>   There are a thousand different ways of getting to work on it. For one thing, there's no 'it'. There's lots of different things. You can think of long-term goals and visions you have in mind, but even if that's what you're focused on, you're going to have to take steps towards them. The steps can be in all kinds of directions, from caring about starving children in Central America or Africa, to working on the rights of working people here, to worrying about the fact that the environment's in serious danger. There's no one thing that's the right thing to do.[29]

> Everything. Everything is a step to take. You organise people; you get them to go on demonstrations; you get them to form political clubs; you get them to beat on the doors of their legislators and the editorial offices; to set up their own newspapers; to make a third party if that's necessary...you form unions. It's all the right thing to do. All of it is right. There are questions of tactics, where you put your efforts. That you just decide. That I can't tell you. But all of these efforts are the right ones.[30]

What is frustrating about Chomsky's response to the question of 'What can we do?' is that he fails to offer arguments for effective strategies for struggle in a context in which so much of the American left has retreated to highly limited forms of reformist politics—such as support for 'lesser evilism' in elections, single-issue lobbying, and consumerist environmentalism—and when he has an enormous audience that is open ·to political suggestions as to how people could radically transform society. It suggests that anything one may choose to do, such as voter registration, is just as good as anything else. Since there is no 'it' (no system) neither history nor theory can provide suggestions as to which strategies are more effective than others for changing the world.

Class analysis

Another important feature of Chomsky's analysis is that his writings and talks offer few examples of successful working class resistance or fightback. In part this can be attributed to the downturn of the 1980s, but it remains the case that Chomsky rarely foregrounds class struggle in concrete terms—successful or unsuccessful strikes, specific strategies or debates in the labour movement, little reported victories of specific workers, or the lessons of labour defeats.[31] When he speaks of 'class struggle', his focus is on the one sided class struggle from above ('the unremitting class war waged by business sectors...on a global scale',[32] which he refers to as having a 'vulgar Marxist' character[33]), not on the specific ways in which workers could more effectively counter the employers' offensive.

Chomsky has certainly pointed to the successful examples of attempts to form class solidarity across ethnic lines during the Homestead Strike, the lively labour press that existed in the United States until it was destroyed in the first half of this century, the more revolutionary beliefs of the mill workers of Massachusetts who understood that 'they who work the mills should own them', and indeed the brutality of the 'one sided class warfare' being waged by bosses against workers. There is no question at all of which side Chomsky is on in these questions. However, there is a tension in Chomsky's work around the issue of effectively organising our forces. On the one hand, Chomsky argues that:

> the overwhelming majority of the population wants to change the 'inherently unfair' economic system, and belief in the basic moral principles of socialism is surprisingly high. What is more, with Soviet tyranny finally overthrown, one long-standing impediment to the realizsation of these ideals is now removed.[34]

Chomsky, though mistaken about how early the Soviet Union became a block to the socialist movement, is certainly right to stress that the collapse of the Stalinist regimes of Eastern Europe is a tremendous advance for the struggle for socialism. And Chomsky is one of the few left intellectuals in the United States to reject the simplistic but widespread belief that the 1994 Republican Congressional election victories represented a massive 'rightward shift' by ordinary working people.[35]

But Chomsky's emphasis on the 'remarkable victory of the doctrinal system', which has 'removed far beyond thought' even 'the minimal conditions for functioning democracy',[36] and diminished the culture of solidarity that existed during the high point of the American labour movement in the early part of this century, overshadows his discussion of possibilities for resistance; it is also difficult to square with the bitterness, political dynamism, and volatility of recent labour struggles (such as the Decatur struggles, Caterpillar, the Detroit newspaper strike, and the successful GM Dayton and Boeing strikes). This is in part the result of Chomsky's repeated emphasis on the success of the 'propaganda system' in curbing popular dissent and 'pacify[ing] the public'.[37]

While he has argued that 'this system [of media control] is not all-powerful',[38] the thrust of his analysis suggests that American 'intellectual culture' has become so bankrupt, the oppositional forces of 'civil society' so fragmented and weak, and the bounds of the doctrinal framework so hard to escape, that there are tremendous grounds for despair.[39] Chomsky observes in a recent account of the attack on American labour:

We cannot really say that the current corporate offensive has driven working class organisation and culture back to the level of a century ago. At that time working people and the poor were nowhere near as isolated nor subject to the ideological monopoly of the business media.[40]

Chomsky would agree that the extent to which the 'system is not functioning' is popularly understood and has increased sharply in recent years, as measured in statistics about alienation and hostility toward established institutions in American society—and the material fact of declining real wages, longer work hours, unsafe jobs, and increased workplace discrimination. Yet the thrust of Chomsky's argument is to suggest that people are so isolated and the propaganda system so overwhelming, that opportunities for raising revolutionary politics are for the most part non-existent. Or, if they do exist, such strategies have no clear priority over other forms of political activism.

It is still the case that Chomsky essentially envisions a 'two-stage picture' of social change: we need first to build a larger reform effort before we can meaningfully undertake more radical social struggles. 'If this two-stage picture is a reasonable one', Rai comments, 'then it is clear that the first priority is to create a coalition of interests and groups, some greater coalescence of single-issue campaigns', rather than to build an organisation that would attempt to organise around revolutionary politics and engage in and try to build a distinctly socialist current in the fight for more immediate reforms.[41] Rai argues that:

> *Chomsky's reluctance to devote effort to 'revolutionary strategy' stems... from his judgment that such work is premature. Talking about such matters is almost meaningless to the bulk of the population. The structure of power means that people's options are radically limited. Furthermore, the propaganda system has to a large extent crushed the capacity for independent thought.*[42]

This is a misguided—and ultimately quite elitist—argument which reflects the pessimism that is, despite his frequent gestures toward possibilities for change, a strong undercurrent in Chomsky's work.

Chomsky on 'humanitarian intervention'

Although Chomsky has distinguished himself especially for his critique of US imperialism and has done more than any other writer to dismantle the myth of 'humanitarian intervention' (most recently opposing the Gulf War and the US invasion of Somalia), he has more recently offered critical support for the intervention of US troops in Haiti and the Balkans.

In neither case did Chomsky support the *doctrine* of 'humanitarian intervention'. In fact, in his writings and lectures on Bosnia and Haiti he has exposed Western economic and military interests, which he sees as the real motivation of the actions. But he has retreated from the logical conclusions of his own arguments because of a lack of confidence in a political alternative. A few months before the US invasion of Haiti, Chomsky argued forcefully:

> *If there's a military intervention, that's the end of any hope for Haitian democracy, absolute end. Maybe the population will get desperate enough so it will even welcome a military intervention. That could happen. But anybody who thinks it's going to bring about democracy just hasn't looked at a history book. Find a case. There's plenty of history of intervention, plenty, including Haiti... The Marines entered Haiti in 1915... They totally destroyed the constitutional system, they reinstituted slavery, they killed a couple of thousand people... The main thing the US did was create a military force to control the population; it didn't have one before... The population was disarmed, the security force was set up to control them. That was 20 years of intervention.*

That's why when you go to Haiti...you talk to people who are really under the whip, and they do not want an American intervention—because they know what it means.[43]

But on the eve of the invasion, Chomsky told the *Boston Globe* that, ' "given the givens", he would invade. "It'll probably cut the terror", he said'.[44] Chomsky cited popular Haitian support for the invasion, though it is clear that the basis of that support was the mistaken belief that the United States was intervening to 'save' Haitians from the Macoutes. 'As Pentagon leaders described it,' the *New York Times* acknowledged, 'their mission is not to protect Haitians from a repressive regime, but to help stabilise the country'.[45] One Haitian politician put the matter quite clearly: 'This is an agreement between the US and the Haitian military, not with the Haitian people'.[46]

The investigative journalist Allan Nairn, who uncovered the CIA sponsorship of the right wing paramilitary organisation Fraph, wrote perceptively in the *Nation* that the aim of the US invasion was 'to prevent the Haitian population from taking politics into its own hands and to forestall the danger of radical mass mobilisation'. Mouvman Peyizan Papay, the largest peasant organisation in Haiti, opposed the US intervention for this reason: 'The occupation will be an invasion against the Haitian people,' explained MPP spokesperson Chavannes Jean-Baptiste, 'and nothing good will come of this for the popular movement'.[47]

The logic of the US intervention was demonstrated soon after the invasion at a march by Haitians on the third anniversary of the 30 September 1991 coup, which overthrew Aristide. At least six demonstrators were killed by paramilitary attaches during the march 'as American soldiers, deployed blocks away in tanks surrounded by barbed wire, did nothing to stop the violence'.

When American troops had first arrived, Haitians in the demonstration 'danced, pulling American flags from their pockets and shouting, "The Americans have truly liberated us!"' But when the American troops 'quickly drove off...the mood grew bitter toward the American soldiers as it became clear that the American force in Haiti, now more than 20,000 strong, would not provide protection to the marchers':

'I can't believe what I see now,' [one demonstrator] said. *'The American soldiers were supposed to be here to help us. They were to restore democracy and protect us from the machine guns of the Fraph people'.*[48]

But, as the *Wall Street Journal* reported, 'Haiti's brutal police and armed military forces remained firmly in control... Haiti's iron-fisted military is still in charge'.[49]

Chomsky's position on the dispatch of troops by the United States and NATO to the Balkans following the Dayton accords followed a similar logic to his support for the Haiti intervention: it was the best of the poor alternatives he saw available. Chomsky told radio journalist David Barsamian in January 1996:

> *I just didn't see any substantive proposals as to what could be done... Now, suppose I had been in Congress, let's say, and had been asked to choose between exactly two alternatives. One, let them keep massacring one another. Two, put in US troops to separate warring armies, to partition the country into two US dependencies with a possibility that something may go badly wrong, as in Somalia, and there might be a huge slaughter. If those are the two choices, I probably would have voted for sending the troops.*[50]

Chomsky is not a member of Congress, and it is disturbing that he should use that analogy and so narrowly restrict his options. Positions other than support for sending US and NATO troops were available, namely supporting steps to build an international solidarity movement against the nationalism of the rival parties in the Balkans and against the calls for military intervention. It is a sign of the current weakness of the Anglo-American left that almost no one, including Chomsky, pointed to such a possibility.[51]

Instead of creating a resolution of the conflict, the US-NATO invasion has served primarily to enforce and institutionalise ethnic cleansing and partition, propping up the brutal regimes of Slobadan Milosevic and Franjo Tudjman while arms flow freely into the still tremendously unstable region. Before the accords, Western intervention had encouraged the greatest act of ethnic cleansing of the war, Croatia's Krajina offensive, which led to hundreds of deaths and displaced over 260,000 Serbs, causing the biggest refugee flow in Europe since the Hungarian uprising was crushed in 1956. The Clinton administration 'gave the green light' to and helped supply arms for Croatia's Krajina offensive,[52] and then 'turned a blind eye to the smuggling of arms from Muslim countries—including Iran—to the Bosnian government'.[53]

Then, under the pretext of the Dayton accords, Clinton announced on 8 July 1996 that 'the American-led effort to train and equip the army of the Muslim-Croat Federation would begin immediately', and arranged for a contract between the federation and Military Professional Resources, Inc, which prepared Croatia for the Krajina offensive. The aid included $100 million of military equipment, including light anti-tank weapons and helicopters, in addition to $140 million pledged by Saudia Arabia and other countries.[54] 'Opposition party members are being terrorised and beaten by agents of the Muslim-dominated government [in Bosnia] in a campaign of intimidation that further erodes any pretense of fairness in the coming...elections,' the *New York Times* acknowledged.[55]

Instead of supporting the dispatch of NATO and US troops, Chomsky was uniquely placed to have raised awareness of the little known examples of working class solidarity, across ethnic lines, during the pre-war strike wave in the Balkans in 1987 and 1991-1992, and to have argued convincingly for the possibility of building a multi-ethnic peace movement in the Balkans and internationally to oppose rival nationalisms and imperialism. The seeds of such a movement existed in the pre-war strike wave, war desertion and resistance, and anti-war demonstrations in Belgrade, Sarajevo, and Zagreb.

The possibility of such a movement can be seen again in the wave of demonstrations that has shaken the Milosevic regime since November 1996 as students and pensioners, joined by workers in Nis and in Belgrade, have taken to the streets in massive numbers to challenge election annulments, restrictions on free speech, and the economic crisis brought on by the war. While led by ultra-nationalist politicians, these demonstrations have begun to mobilise the kind of anti-nationalist sentiment that could have far more impact than NATO and US troops on the level of inter-ethnic warfare, ethnic cleansing, and suffering in the Balkans—particularly if they addressed the concerns of workers whose standard of living has drastically declined as a result of the war and the collapse of state capitalism in the Balkans.

Part of the reason that Chomsky has not reached this judgement is that he has accepted a narrow definition of the options available to the left and has isolated these cases from the urgency of rebuilding an anti-imperialist movement in the United States.[56] It is increasingly clear that only such a movement can begin to mount the kind of challenge that could, in Chomsky's own phrase, 'raise the costs of state intervention' (as was done during the Vietnam War), create a larger space for the many people trying to organise under the boot of US imperialism, and offer the possibility of ending war altogether.

Chomsky on Marxism

Though the Marxist tradition has developed the most theoretically and practically incisive analysis of the economy, war, social relations under capitalism, and the means for achieving socialism, Chomsky has frequently suggested that it has little beyond 'trivial' insights to offer. He has on several occasions identified positively with aspects of the 'left Marxist' tradition, in which he includes figures such as Rosa Luxemburg, the Dutch council communists Anton Pannekoek and Herman Gorter, and Paul Mattick, but his work reflects little engagement

with the classical Marxist tradition, including Luxemburg, and his pro-
nouncements on Marxism generally have been dismissive:

> *Marxism in my view belongs in the history of organised religion. In fact, as a*
> *rule of thumb, any concept with a person's name on it belongs to religion, not*
> *rational discourse... That means, if you identify yourself as a Marxist or a*
> *Freudian, or anything else, you're worshipping at someone's shrine.*
>
> *If the field of social and historical and economic analysis was so trivial*
> *that what somebody wrote a hundred years ago could still be authoritative,*
> *you might as well talk about some other topic. But as I understand Marx, he*
> *constructed a somewhat interesting theory of a rather abstract model of 19th*
> *century capitalism. He did good journalism. And he had interesting ideas*
> *about history. He probably had about five sentences in his entire body of work*
> *about what a postcapitalist society is supposed to look like.*[57]

Chomsky told Robert McChesney:

> *I haven't really been a critic of Marxism. I largely ignore it. I'm frankly scep-*
> *tical of what are called 'theories' in the study of social and political issues, or*
> *just about anything of real and direct human significance... As for Marxism,*
> *the early Marx was interesting, but pretty derivative... The later Marx offers*
> *vivid and enlightening commentary...[but] [h]e appears to have little to say*
> *about socialism, and little interest in it.*[58]

Setting aside Marx's important commentaries on the relevance of the
Paris Commune for defining a vision of a future socialist society, and his
lifelong commitment to building such a society,[59] what is striking in
Chomsky's comments is his failure to take up even the most basic
premises of Marxism—premises which remain tremendously relevant
today as a set of living ideas, tested in practice, about the nature of capitalist society and how workers can organise to achieve their self
emancipation.

It is precisely this idea, that the working class must be the agent of its
own 'self emancipation' and that socialism can only come *from below*,
that is the unique and lasting contribution of Marxism. In contrast to the
common idea that Marxism holds a Blanquist theory of the seizure of
state power by a small minority, Marx argued clearly in the *Communist
Manifesto* that socialism is for the first time 'the self conscious, independent movement of the immense majority' which will take power 'in the
interest of the immense majority'.[60]

The point of theory is not to elaborate more theory or to dress up
simple ideas in complex academic language. It is to help inform the
practice of those struggling to change the world. If one is not a Marxist,

it is not that one has no 'theory in the study of social and political issues'; one simply has another theory, whether of capitalism, oppression, racism, sexism, homophobia, the market or movements for national liberation.[61]

Chomsky on Bolshevism

While merely dismissive of Marxism, Chomsky has been a virulent critic of Bolshevism, Leninism and of the Russian Revolution, at times echoing far right rhetoric. To take one of many examples, according to Chomsky:

> *The Bolshevik coup of October 1917 placed state power in the hands of Lenin and Trotsky, who moved quickly to dismantle the incipient socialist institutions that had grown up during the popular revolution of the preceding months—the factory councils, the Soviets, in fact any organ of popular control... In any meaningful sense of the term 'socialism', the Bolsheviks moved at once to destroy its existing elements.*[62]

In one of his most recent books, Chomsky refers to the 'two major forms of 20th century totalitarianism, Fascism and Bolshevism'.[63] Such anti-Leninist and anti-Bolshevik passages occur throughout Chomsky's writings and interviews, going back to his first essays.[64]

In Chomsky's view, Lenin's theory of the party is based on the idea that 'the public, especially the working class, are too stupid to know what's good for them':[65]

> *Lenin's idea was that you have a group of revolutionary intellectuals, who are the smart guys, and they're to drive the society to a better future, which the Slavs are too dumb to understand. That's basically the idea, which is not all that different from the ideology of capitalist democracy.*[66]

Indeed, Chomsky has compared the ideology of Lenin with that of Robert McNamara,[67] one of the leading forces behind the Vietnam War.

What characterises Chomsky's attacks on Leninism and Bolshevism, beyond their virulence, is a surprising lack of intellectual or scholarly engagement with the actual history or theory of the Bolshevik tradition. Thus, for example, Chomsky claims that 'the Bolshevik takeover was recognised as an attack on socialism very quickly by a large part of the left...[including] Rosa Luxemburg',[68] a completely inaccurate statement, as even a swift glance at Luxemburg's writings shows. Despite the heated and important debates between Luxemburg, Trotsky, and Lenin, she was very clear that:

The party of Lenin was...the only one in Russia which grasped the true interest of the revolution in that first period. It was the element which drove the revolution forward, and, thus, it was the only party which really carried on a socialist policy... [T]he Bolsheviks, though they were at the beginning of the revolution a persecuted, slandered and hunted minority attacked on all sides, arrived within the shortest time to the head of the revolution and were able to bring under their banner all the genuine masses of the people: the urban proletariat, the army, the peasants, as well as the revolutionary elements of democracy.[69]

All the revolutionary honour and capacity which western social democracy lacked were represented by the Bolsheviks. Their October uprising was not only the actual salvation of the Russian Revolution; it was the salvation of the honour of international socialism.[70]

And while she made clear her concerns about decisions made by the Bolshevik leadership after October, she stressed the catastrophically difficult political circumstances in which the Bolsheviks found themselves.[71] Chomsky's discussion of the Russian Revolution, however, consistently passes over the issues raised by Luxemburg: the impact of the civil war and the imperialist interventions that quickly followed the revolution, the failure of revolutions in Germany and elsewhere to succeed in building international support for the Russian working class, and the economic crisis which had a severe impact on Russian workers and peasants, the base of the October uprising.

In striking contrast to his highly documented work on almost every other subject, Chomsky provides little evidence of sources or documents to support his position, even though most serious historical work on the revolution makes it clear that it was not a coup by the Bolsheviks, but a revolution from below, entirely dependent on the Bolsheviks having become the majority within the soviets.

As the work of those historians who have looked at the revolution 'from below' has convincingly argued, the view of the Bolshevik Revolution as a coup by a small, dictatorial party does not stand up to examination.[72] 'Historians in the Soviet Union have stressed historical inevitability and the role of a tightly knit revolutionary party led by Lenin in accounting for the outcome of the October Revolution, while many Western scholars have viewed this event either as a historical accident or, more frequently, as the result of a well-executed *coup d'état* without significant mass support,' Alexander Rabinowitch argues, but:

a full explanation of the Bolshevik seizure of power is much more complex than any of these interpretations suggest.

> *Studying the aspirations of factory workers, soldiers, and sailors as expressed in contemporary documents... these concerns corresponded closely to the programme of political, economic, and social reform put forth by the Bolsheviks at a time when all other major political parties were discredited because of their failure to press hard enough for meaningful internal changes and an immediate end to Russia's participation in the [First World] War. As a result, in October, the goals of the Bolsheviks, as the masses understood them, had strong popular support.*
>
> *In Petrograd in 1917 the Bolshevik Party bore little resemblance to the by-and-large united, authoritarian, conspiratorial organisation effectively controlled by Lenin depicted in most accounts.*[73]

The idea that the revolution was a coup was also challenged at the time by non-Bolshevik writers, such as the Menshevik Nikolai Sukhanov.[74]

One central element of Chomsky's critique is that the Bolsheviks were hostile towards and later destroyed the soviets because of their elitist attitude toward the working class. Beyond the many arguments directly contradicting this view in Lenin's *State and Revolution* and, indeed, later work[75]—which Chomsky argues was 'all a fraud'[76]—even the strongly anti-Bolshevik historian Oskar Anweiler acknowledges that 'aside from the Bolsheviks, only the small group of United Social Democrats supported the demand for soviet power'. The Mensheviks' and SR's:

> *rejection of Soviet power hardened during the following months* [after June 1917]. *Especially after the July Days laid bare the split within 'revolutionary democracy', there prevailed, in Kerensky's words, 'the conviction among soviet leaders that the soviets were not and could not be governing organs but that they were merely tools for transition to a new democratic order'. Kerensky himself assured the British ambassador, Sir George Buchanan, as early as May: 'The soviets will die a natural death'...*[and] *the Mensheviks saw no future for the soviets... [A]lmost daily the balance in the local soviets shifted in favour of the Bolsheviks and their call for sole soviet power... Unlike parties which had majorities in earlier soviets, the Bolsheviks proposed specifically that future soviets should seize power in their own name and build a state on their own pattern.*[77]

Thus, as Moshe Lewin suggests,

> *Leninist doctrine did not originally envisage a monolithic state, nor even a strictly monolithic party; the dictatorship of the party over the proletariat was never part of Lenin's plans, it was the completely unforeseen culmination of a series of unforeseen circumstances.*[78]

The isolation, crisis, and then destruction of socialism under the Stalinist counter-revolution have been well documented,[79] but the argument that Lenin and the Bolsheviks instituted a dictatorship through a 'revolution from above' does not hold up under examination.

Chomsky, however, sees the revolutionary, or 'vanguard', party as *inevitably* substitutionist and elitist, putting itself in the place of the working class and acting 'on its behalf'. In contrast, the tradition of socialism from below argues that there is a mutual relationship between the organised and most politically conscious political section of the working class, the party, which seeks to organise other workers and win them to revolutionary politics through argument and through concrete activity in the workplace and outside it in which party and class must educate and learn from one another. The party is not the future ruling class of a state, or a directing dictatorial body, but that section of the working class which is most politically and class conscious and which seeks to argue, agitate, and mobilise for *mass working class struggle and self-activity*.

Indeed, Luxemburg, Pannekoek and Gorter all agreed at key moments on the need for exactly such a party. Pannekoek noted, 'The function of a revolutionary party lies in propagating clear understanding in advance, so that throughout the masses there will be elements who know what must be done and who are capable of judging the situation for themselves',[80] while Gorter argued for the need 'to unite [the] section of the proletariat that has a large and profound understanding within one organisation... [to] overcome or relieve all the weaknesses...to which the factory organisation is subject'.[81]

Conclusion

As Gareth Jenkins has argued, Noam Chomsky's 'brilliance in exposing the lies, evasions, and hypocrisies of ruling class double think... is unparalleled and has...earned [him] the hatred of what Marx called the intellectual prizefighters of the world's oppressors'.[82] As Robert Barsky, Chomsky's biographer, points out, 'He was, and is, for generations of dissenters a figure of enlightenment and inspiration'.[83] But Chomsky's anarchism and his rejection of the Marxist tradition present serious limitations. Thus, Jenkins notes, 'while it is clear whose side [Chomsky] is on, it is not clear that he has a strategy for victory against the forces both he and we hate'.[84]

In Barsky's words, 'There remains, at the end of the event, the problem of "how to take on the bastards".'[85] While there is a tremendous amount that socialists can learn and take from Chomsky's work, we clearly need to critically engage and challenge his ideas in many cases and most urgently—set about building an organisation that provides 'a strategy for victory'. The task of building a revolutionary socialist party today is vital. The welcome collapse of Stalinism and the false socialist regimes of Eastern Europe clears away an immense amount of rubbish and makes it easier than it has been in decades for revolutionaries to rebuild the genuine tradition of socialism from below.

Notes

I would like to thank Paul D'Amato, Stuart Easterling, Bosse Ekelund, Phil Gasper, Anna Kuperman, Marlene Martin, Joe Nevins, Nagesh Rao, Lance Selfa, Ashley Smith, Elizabeth Terzakis, and especially Noam Chomsky for their comments on earlier versions of this essay.

1   N Chomsky, 'The Responsibility of Intellectuals', *American Power and the New Mandarins: Historical and Political Essays* (New York, 1969), p313. See also N Chomsky, *At War with Asia* (New York, 1970).

2   N Chomsky, *The Fateful Triangle: The United States, Israel, and the Palestinians* (Boston, 1983), p468.

3   N Chomsky, *World Orders Old and New*, 2nd edn (New York, 1996), p252; see also pp189-297.

4   The reviewer then adds that, despite his brilliance as a linguist, Chomsky's 'substantial body of political writings' is 'maddeningly simple-minded'. *The New York Times Book Review*, 25 February 1979, quoted in P Wintonick and M Achbar, *Manufacturing Consent: Noam Chomsky and the Media* (London, 1994), p19.

5   N Chomsky, *Chomsky Reader*, J Peck (ed) (New York, 1987), p13.

6   N Chomsky, *Class Warfare: Interviews with David Barsamian* (Monroe, 1996), p93.

7   Ibid.

8   Quoted in M Rai, *Chomsky's Politics* (London, 1995), p7.

9   Quoted in ibid, p8.

10   Quoted in ibid, pp8-9.

11   See N Chomsky, *Chomsky Reader*, op cit, pp85-119.

12   The Stalinists' role in Spain runs completely counter to Lenin and Trotsky's ideas of internationalism and socialism from below. See, for example, Trotsky's 19 February 1937 statement on the Spanish Civil War: 'In Spain the Stalinists, who lead the chorus from on high, have advanced the formula to which Caballero, president of the cabinet, also adheres: *First* military victory, and *then* social reform. I consider this formula fatal for the Spanish Revolution... *Audacious social reforms represent the strongest weapon in the civil war and the fundamental condition for the victory over fascism.* The policies of Stalin...are dictated by a fear of frightening the French bourgeoisie' (L Trotsky, *The Spanish Revolution (1931-39)* N Allen and G Breitman (eds) (New York, 1973), pp242-243.

13   N Chomsky, *Chomsky Reader*, op cit, p90.

14   Ibid, p13.

15   Ibid, p14.

16   N Chomsky, quoted in R F Barsky, *Noam Chomsky: A Life of Dissent* (London, 1997), p80.

17   See, for example, N Chomsky, *Cartesian Linguistics: A Chapter in the History of Rationalist Thought* (London, 1966). More recent statements on this subject can

be found in N Chomsky, *Powers and Prospects: Reflections on Human Nature and the Social Order* (Boston, 1996), pp1-54, and *Language and Thought* (London, 1993).

18   See Chomsky's 8 August 1994 letter to Barsky: 'I think there is an important and detectable "thread"... that runs from Cartesian rationalism through the romantic period (the more libertarian Rousseau, for example), parts of the enlightenment (some of Kant, etc), pre-capitalist classical liberalism (notably Humboldt, but also [Adam] Smith), and on to the partly spontaneous tradition of popular revolt against industrial capitalism and the forms it took in the left-libertarian movements, including the anti-Bolshevik parts of the Marxist tradition.' Quoted in R F Barsky, *Noam Chomsky: A Life of Dissent*, op cit, p107; cf pp102-116, especially pp112-113; N Chomsky, *Class Warfare*, op cit, p29; and N Chomsky, *World Orders Old and New*, op cit, pp86-87.

      On anarchism, generally, see N Chomsky, 'Notes on Anarchism', *For Reasons of State* (New York, 1973), pp370-386; *Radical Priorities* 2nd ed, C P Otero (ed) (Montréal, 1981), pp245-261; *Language and Politics*, C P Otero (ed) (Montréal, 1988), pp166-197; and 'Goals and Visions', *Powers and Prospects* , op cit, pp70-93.

19   S Pinker, *The Language Instinct: How the Mind Creates Language* (New York, 1995), pp21-22.

20   N Chomsky, *The Minimalist Program* (London, 1995), p2.

21   Ibid, p11, fn 16.

22   N Chomsky, *Aspects of the Theory of Syntax* (Cambridge, 1965), p3. While Chomsky is undertaking a methodological abstraction here, there is a vital tradition of linguistics which has attempted to approach the question of language and expression from a historical materialist standpoint. See, in particular, V N Volosinov, *Marxism and the Philosophy of Language*, trans L Matejka and I R Titunik (London, 1986); and M N Bakhtin and P N Medvedev, *The Formal Method in Literary Scholarship: A Critical Introduction to Sociological Poetics* (London, 1991).

23   R F Barsky, *Noam Chomsky: A Life of Dissent*, op cit, p137.

24   Ibid, pp122 and 131.

25   31 March 1995 letter to Barsky in ibid, p131. See also N Chomsky, 'Knowledge and Power: Intellectuals and the Welfare/Warfare State', in P Long (ed), *The New Left: A Collection of Essays* (Boston, 1969), pp172-199, and *Radical Priorities*, op cit, pp218-243, which include critiques of apsects of the student movement.

26   See Chomsky's comments on his participation in Resist in N Chomsky, *Class Warfare*, op cit, pp56-57.

27   M Rai, *Chomsky's Politics*, op cit, pp21 and 49.

28   N Chomsky, *Secrets, Lies and Democracy* (Tuscan, 1994), pp105-106.

29   N Chomsky, *Class Warfare* pp114-115.

30   N Chomsky, 'Noam Chomsky: An Interview', by B Lesseraux (Coalition Press, 1995), p10. Chomsky here echoes Eduard Bernstein's revisionist argument that 'the movement is everything', which forms the starting point of Rosa Luxemburg's brilliant, and still remarkably relevant, critique of revisionism in *Reform or Revolution* (London, 1989), p21. Chomsky does not argue that 'The final goal, no matter what it is, is nothing' (p21), but he certainly would agree with the Bernsteinian idea that socialists 'should build socialism by means of the progressive extension of social control and the gradual application of the principle of cooperation' (p26). See Chomsky's argument that 'the left if it is serious is going to have to create the facts of the future within the institutional structures of the present' (R McChesney, 'An Interview with Noam Chomsky: On Media, Politics and the Left, Part I', *Against the Current* 10:1 (March-April 1995), p31).

31   For a recent example of Chomsky's views on labour politics, see 'The Third
      World at Home', *Year 501: The Conquest Continues* (London, 1993), pp275-288.
32   N Chomsky, *World Orders Old and New*, op cit, p158.
33   N Chomsky, *Class Warfare*, op cit, p17.
34   N Chomsky, *Year 501:*, op cit (London, 1993), p286.
35   See, for example, J Hardisty, 'The Resurgent Right: Why Now?' *The Public Eye*
      9:3/4 (Fall/Winter 1995). Hardisty argues that the 1994 'election results indicate
      that the American public has repudiated the liberalism that has been the dominant
      method of social reform since the New Deal. The resurgent right has consolidated
      its power and is now implementing its agenda' (p1). 'The average voter...[has]
      been won over to the right's agenda' (p3). For a much clearer view of the election
      results, see T Ferguson, *The Golden Rule: The Investment Theory of Party
      Competition and the Logic of Money-Driven Political Systems* (Chicago, 1995),
      pp359-375; H Zinn, *A People's History of the United States: 1492 to Present*,
      revised edition (New York, 1995), pp633-634; and N Chomsky, 'Rollback', in *The
      New American Crisis: Radical Analyses of the Problems Facing America Today*,
      G Ruggiero and S Sahulka (eds) (New York, 1995), pp11-30.
36   N Chomsky, *Year 501*, op cit, p276.
37   N Chomsky, *World Orders Old and New*, op cit, p120.
38   E S Herman and N Chomsky, *Manufacturing Consent: The Political Economy of
      the Mass Media* (New York, 1988), p306. See C Nineham, 'Is the Media All
      Powerful?' *International Socialism* 67.
39   'The answer is to rebuild civil society', Chomsky said in a recent interview when
      asked how it was possible to fight for the social reforms won by labour struggles
      of the 1930s, now being destroyed by Clinton and the Gingrich Republicans
      (J Walljasper, 'Left Behind?' *The Providence Phoenix* (27 September 1996), p20).
40   N Chomsky, *Year 501*, op cit, p285.
41   M Rai, *Chomsky's Politics*, op cit, p110.
42   Ibid, p123.
43   'Orwell's World and Ours', 16 June 1994 lecture to Z Media Institute (audiotape).
44   *Boston Globe*, 18 September 1994.
45   *New York Times*, 21 September 1994.
46   Ibid.
47   Quoted in A Nairn, 'The Eagle is Landing', *The Nation* 259:10 (3 October 1994),
      p344. See also C Jean-Baptiste, 'Tying Aristide's Hands', *The Progressive* 58:9
      (September 1994), p26.
48   *New York Times*, 21 September 1994.
49   *Wall Street Journal*, 21 September 1994.
50   N Chomsky, *Class Warfare*, op cit, pp160-161.
51   See L German, 'The Balkan War: Can There Be Peace?' and D Blackie, 'The Left
      and the Balkan War', *International Socialism* 69, for a fuller account of this
      argument. See also C. Kimber 'Defying the Dictators', *Socialist Review* 204
      (January 1997), pp14-15; and D. Blackie, 'The Road to Hell', *International
      Socialism* 53.
52   *New York Times*, 28 October 1995.
53   *New York Times*, 25 May 1996.
54   *New York Times*, 9 July 1996.
55   *New York Times*, 17 August 1996.
56   See, for example, N Chomsky, 'On Intervention', *Boston Review* 19:6 (December-
      January 1993-1994), p7: 'We can, in short, ask whether the pursuit of self-interest
      [by a state] might happen to benefit others in particular cases.'
57   C M Young, 'Anarchy in the USA', *Rolling Stone* 631 (28 May 1992), p47.
58   R McChesney, 'The Media, Politics and Ourselves: Interview with Noam
      Chomsky, Part 2', *Against the Current* 56 (May-June 1995), p25.

59   See K Marx and F Engels, *Writings on the Paris Commune*, H Draper (ed) (London, 1971).

60   K Marx and F Engels, *The Communist Manifesto*, (London, 1995), p92. See Hal Draper's brilliant 'The Principle of Self-Emancipation in Marx and Engels', in E Haberkern (ed), *Socialism from Below* (London, 1992), pp243-271. Also H Draper, *Karl Marx's Theory of Revolution*, 4 vols (New York, 1977-1990), especially vols 1 and 4, and *The Two Souls of Socialism*, (London, 1996).

61   For example, in response to David Barsamian's question, 'Some Marxists connect racism as a product of the economic system, of capitalism. Would you accept that?' Chomsky replies, 'No. It has to do with conquest' (N Chomsky, *Keeping the Rabble in Line: Interviews with David Barsamian* (Monroe, 1994), pp93-94. This is a 'theory' of race, one which has to present its merits and offer itself up for comparison with a Marxist theory. See, for example, A Callinicos, *Race and Class* (London, 1992).

62   N Chomsky, *What Uncle Sam Really Wants* (Berkeley, 1993), p91.

63   N Chomsky, *Powers and Prospects*, op cit, p73.

64   See, for example, N Chomsky, 'The Soviet Union vs Socialism', *Our Generation* 17:2 (Spring-Summer 1986), pp47-52; note, in particular, his reference to 'the intense hostility to socialism on the part of the Leninist intelligentsia (*with roots in Marx, no doubt*)' (p52; emphasis added). For a critique of the Bakuninist myth that Marx destroyed the First International because of his hostility to working people, see H Draper, *Karl Marx's Theory of Revolution*, vol 4 (New York, 1990), pp270-304.

65   N Chomsky: 'An Interview', *Radical Philosophy* 53 (Autumn 1989), p38.

66   C M Young, 'Anarchy in the USA', op cit, p47.

67   N Chomsky, *Towards a New Cold War* (New York, 1982), pp63-64.

68   N Chomsky, *World Orders Old and New*, op cit, p38.

69   R Luxemburg, *Rosa Luxemburg Speaks* (London, 1994), p372.

70   Ibid, p375.

71   See ibid, pp394-395.

72   For a useful review of some of the literature on the revolution, including the work of the revisionists, see D Howl, 'Bookwatch: The Russian Revolution', *International Socialism* 62.

73   A Rabinowitch, *The Bolsheviks Come to Power: The Revolution of 1917 in Petrograd* (London, 1976), pxvii. See also D H Kaiser (ed), *The Workers' Revolution in 1917: The View from Below* (Cambridge, 1987).

74   N N Sukhanov, *The Russian Revolution 1917: A Personal Record* (Princeton, 1984), pp648-649. See also H Mendel, *Memoirs of a Jewish Revolutionary* (London, 1989), p164.

75   See, for example, V I Lenin, *State and Revolution* (London, 1992), pp78-79, 91-92, and 96; and P LeBlanc, *Lenin and the Revolutionary Party* (London, 1990), p299.

76   'Noam Chomsky: An Interview', *Radical Philosophy*, op cit, p39.

77   O Anweiler, *The Soviets: The Russian Workers, Peasants, and Soldiers Councils, 1905-1921*, trans R Hein (New York, 1974), pp141-143. See also E Acton, 'The Libertarians Vindicated? The Libertarian View of the Revolution in the Light of Recent Western Research', in E R Frankel et al (ed), *Revolution in Russia: Reassessments of 1917*, (Cambridge, 1992), p401. See also W G Rosenberg, 'Russian Labour and Bolshevik Power: Social Dimensions of Protest in Petrograd after October', in R G Suny (ed), *The Workers' Revolution in Russia, 1917*, pp98-131.

78   M Lewin, *Lenin's Last Struggle* (Monthly Review Press, 1968), p17.

79   See J Rees, 'In Defence of October', *International Socialism* 52, and the discussion that follows in *International Socialism* 55.

80   A Pannekoek, 'World Revolution and Communist Tactics' (1920), in D A Smart (ed), *Pannekoek and Gorter's Marxism* (London, 1978), pp100-101. I owe this reference to Paul LeBlanc. See P LeBlanc, *Lenin and the Revolutionary Party*, pp291-292, for a gloss on the Gorter and Pannekoek quotes. See K Marx and F Engels, *The Communist Manifesto*, pp95-96, op cit, on the relationship between 'proletarians and Communists.' See also J Molyneux, *Marxism and the Party* (London, 1978), and T Cliff et al, *Party and Class,* 2nd ed (London, 1996).

81   H Gorter 'The Organisation of the Proletariat's Class Struggle' (1921), in Pannekoek and Gorter's Marxism, op cit, p161. Gorter stresses: '[T]he question poses itself as to whether [trade union] organisation is sufficient, whether a political Communist Party is also necessary... [T]he whole revolution depends just as much upon the answer we give to it as upon what organisation can make the great majority of the proletariat into conscious militants' (p158). His clear answer is that such a party is indeed necessary.

82   G Jenkins, 'Honour and Anger Are Not Enough', *International Socialism* 53, p120.

83   R F Barsky, *Noam Chomsky: A Life of Dissent*, op cit, p191.

84   G Jenkins, 'Honour and Anger Are Not Enough', op cit, p120.

85   R F Barsky, *Noam Chomsky: A Life of Dissent*, op cit, p217.

The Socialist Workers Party is one of an international grouping of socialist organisations:

AUSTRALIA: International Socialists, PO Box A338, Sydney South

BELGIUM: Socialisme International, Rue Lovinfosse 60, 4030 Grivengée, Belgium

BRITAIN: Socialist Workers Party, PO Box 82, London E3

CANADA: International Socialists, PO Box 339, Station E, Toronto, Ontario M6H 4E3

CYPRUS: Ergatiki Demokratia, PO Box 7280, Nicosia

DENMARK: Internationale Socialister, Postboks 642, 2200 København N, Denmark

FRANCE: Socialisme International, BP 189, 75926 Paris Cedex 19

GREECE: Sosialistiko Ergatiko Komma, c/o Workers Solidarity, PO Box 8161, Athens 100 10, Greece

HOLLAND: International Socialists, PO Box 9720, 3506 GR Utrecht

IRELAND: Socialist Workers Movement, PO Box 1648, Dublin 8

NEW ZEALAND:
Socialist Workers Organization, PO Box 8851, Auckland

NORWAY: Internasjonale Socialisterr, Postboks 5370, Majorstua, 0304 Oslo 3

POLAND: Solidarność Socjalistyczna, PO Box 12, 01-900 Warszawa 118

SOUTH AFRICA:
International Socialists of South Africa, PO Box 18530, Hillbrow 2038, Johannesberg

SPAIN: Socialismo Internacional, Apartado 563, 08080, Barcelona

UNITED STATES:
International Socialist Organisation, PO Box 16085, Chicago, Illinois 60616

ZIMBABWE:
International Socialist Organisation, PO Box 6758, Harare

The following issues of *International Socialism* (second series) are available price £3 (including postage) from IS Journal, PO Box 82, London E3 3LH. *International Socialism* 2:58 and 2:65 are available on cassette from the Royal National Institute for the Blind (Peterborough Library Unit). Phone 01733 370777.

International Socialism 2:73 Winter 1996
Chris Harman: Globalisation: a critique of a new orthodoxy ★ Chris Bambery: Marxism and sport ★ John Parrington: Computers and consciousness: a reply to Alex Callinicos ★ Joe Faith: Dennett, materialism and empiricism ★ Megan Trudell: Who made the American Revolution? ★ Mark O'Brien: The class conflicts which shaped British history ★ John Newsinger: From class war to Cold War ★ Alex Callinicos: The state in debate ★ Charlie Kimber: Review article: coming to terms with barbarism in Rwanda in Burundi★

International Socialism 2:72 Autumn 1996
Alex Callinicos: Betrayal and discontent: Labour under Blair ★ Sue Cockerill and Colin Sparks: Japan in crisis ★ Richard Levins: When science fails us ★ Ian Birchall: The Babeuf bicentenary: conspiracy or revolutionary party? ★ Brian Manning: A voice for the poor ★ Paul O'Flinn: From the kingdom of necessity to the kingdom of freedom: Morris's *News from Nowhere* ★ Clare Fermont: Bookwatch: Palestine and the Middle East 'peace process'★

International Socialism 2:71 Summer 1996
Chris Harman: The crisis of bourgeois economics ★ Hassan Mahamdallie: William Morris and revolutionary Marxism ★ Alex Callinicos: Darwin, materialism and revolution ★ Chris Nineham: Raymond Williams: revitalising the left? ★ Paul Foot: A passionate prophet of liberation ★ Gill Hubbard: Why has feminism failed women? ★ Lee Sustar: Bookwatch: fighting to unite black and white★

International Socialism 2:70 Spring 1996
Alex Callinicos: South Africa after apartheid ★ Chris Harman: France's hot December ★ Brian Richardson: The making of a revolutionary ★ Gareth Jenkins: Why Lucky Jim turned right—an obituary of Kingsley Amis ★ Mark O'Brien: The bloody birth of capitalism ★ Lee Humber: Studies in revolution ★ Adrian Budd: A new life for Lenin ★ Martin Smith: Bookwatch: the General Strike★

International Socialism 2:69 Winter 1995
Lindsey German: The Balkan war: can there be peace? ★ Duncan Blackie: The left and the Balkan war ★ Nicolai Gentchev: The myth of welfare dependency ★ Judy Cox: Wealth, poverty and class in Britain today ★ Peter Morgan: Trade unions and strikes ★ Julie Waterson: The party at its peak ★ Megan Trudell: Living to some purpose ★ Nick Howard: The rise and fall of socialism in one city ★ Andy Durgan: Bookwatch: Civil war and revolution in Spain ★

International Socialism 2:68 Autumn 1995
Ruth Brown: Racism and immigration in Britain ★ John Molyneux: Is Marxism deterministic? ★ Stuart Hood: News from nowhere? ★ Lee Sustar: Communism in the heart of the beast ★ Peter Linebaugh: To the teeth and forehead of our faults ★ George Paizis: Back to the future ★ Phil Marshall: The children of stalinism ★ Paul D'Amato: Bookwatch: 100 years of cinema ★

International Socialism 2:67 Summer 1995
Paul Foot: When will the Blair bubble burst? ★ Chris Harman: From Bernstein to Blair—100 years of revisionism ★ Chris Bambery: Was the Second World War a war for democracy? ★ Chris Nineham: Is the media all powerful? ★ Peter Morgan: How the West was won ★ Charlie Hore: Bookwatch: China since Mao ★

International Socialism 2:66 Spring 1995
Dave Crouch: The crisis in Russia and the rise of the right ★ Phil Gasper: Cruel and unusual punishment: the politics of crime in the United States ★ Alex Callinicos: Backwards to liberalism ★ John Newsinger: Matewan: film and working class struggle ★ John Rees: The light and the dark ★ Judy Cox: How to make the Tories disappear ★ Charlie Hore: Jazz: a reply to the critics ★ Pat Riordan: Bookwatch: Ireland ★

International Socialism 2:65 Special Issue
Lindsey German: Frederick Engels: life of a revolutionary ★ John Rees: Engels' Marxism ★ Chris

International Socialism 2:54 Spring 1992

Sharon Smith: Twilight of the American dream ★ Mike Haynes: Class and crisis—the transition in eastern Europe ★ Costas Kossis: A miracle without end? Japanese capitalism and the world economy ★ Alex Callinicos: Capitalism and the state system: A reply to Nigel Harris ★ Steven Rose: Do animals have rights? ★ John Charlton: Crime and class in the 18th century ★ John Rees: Revolution, reform and working class culture ★ Chris Harman: Blood simple ★

International Socialism 2:52 Autumn 1991

John Rees: In defence of October ★ Ian Taylor and Julie Waterson: The political crisis in Greece—an interview with Maria Styllou and Panos Garganas ★ Paul McGarr: Mozart, overture to revolution ★ Lee Humber: Class, class consciousness and the English Revolution ★ Derek Howl: The legacy of Hal Draper ★

International Socialism 2:51 Summer 1991

Chris Harman: The state and capitalism today ★ Alex Callinicos: The end of nationalism? ★ Sharon Smith: Feminists for a strong state? ★ Colin Sparks and Sue Cockerill: Goodbye to the Swedish miracle ★ Simon Phillips: The South African Communist Party and the South African working class ★ John Brown: Class conflict and the crisis of feudalism ★

International Socialism 2:49 Winter 1990

Chris Bambery: The decline of the Western Communist Parties ★ Ernest Mandel: A theory which has not withstood the test of time ★ Chris Harman: Criticism which does not withstand the test of logic ★ Derek Howl: The law of value in the USSR ★ Terry Eagleton: Shakespeare and the class struggle ★ Lionel Sims: Rape and pre-state societies ★ Sheila McGregor: A reply to Lionel Sims ★

International Socialism 2:48 Autumn 1990

Lindsey German: The last days of Thatcher ★ John Rees: The new imperialism ★ Neil Davidson and Donny Gluckstein: Nationalism and the class struggle in Scotland ★ Paul McGarr: Order out of chaos ★

International Socialism 2:46 Winter 1989

Chris Harman: The storm breaks ★ Alex Callinicos: Can South Africa be reformed? ★ John Saville: Britain, the Marshall Plan and the Cold War ★ Sue Clegg: Against the stream ★ John Rees: The rising bourgeoisie ★

International Socialism 2:44 Autumn 1989

Charlie Hore: China: Tiananmen Square and after ★ Sue Clegg: Thatcher and the welfare state ★ John Molyneux: *Animal Farm* revisited ★ David Finkel: After Arias, is the revolution over? ★ John Rose: Jews in Poland ★

International Socialism 2:43 Summer 1989 (Reprint—special price £4.50)

Marxism and the Great French Revolution by Paul McGarr and Alex Callinicos

International Socialism 2:42 Spring 1989

Chris Harman: The myth of market socialism ★ Norah Carlin: Roots of gay oppression ★ Duncan Blackie: Revolution in science ★ International Socialism Index ★

International Socialism 2:41 Winter 1988

Polish socialists speak out: Solidarity at the Crossroads ★ Mike Haynes: Nightmares of the market ★ Jack Robertson: Socialists and the unions ★ Andy Strouthous: Are the unions in decline? ★ Richard Bradbury: What is Post-Structuralism? ★ Colin Sparks: George Bernard Shaw ★

International Socialism 2:39 Summer 1988

Chris Harman and Andy Zebrowski: Glasnost, before the storm ★ Chanie Rosenberg: Labour and the fight against fascism ★ Mike Gonzalez: Central America after the Peace Plan ★ Ian Birchall: Raymond Williams ★ Alex Callinicos: Reply to John Rees ★

International Socialism 2:35 Summer 1987

Pete Green: Capitalism and the Thatcher years ★ Alex Callinicos: Imperialism, capitalism and the state today ★ Ian Birchall: Five years of *New Socialist* ★ Callinicos and Wood debate 'Looking for alternatives to reformism' ★ David Widgery replies on 'Beating Time' ★

International Socialism 2:31 Winter 1985

Alex Callinicos: Marxism and revolution in South Africa ★ Tony Cliff: The tragedy of A J Cook ★ Nigel Harris: What to do with London? The strategies of the GLC ★

International Socialism 2:30 Autumn 1985
Gareth Jenkins: Where is the Labour Party heading? ★ David McNally: Debt, inflation and the rate of profit ★ Ian Birchall: The terminal crisis in the British Communist Party ★ replies on Women's oppression and *Marxism Today* ★

International Socialism 2:29 Summer 1985
Special issue on the class struggle and the left in the aftermath of the miners' defeat ★ Tony Cliff: Patterns of mass strike ★ Chris Harman: 1984 and the shape of things to come ★ Alex Callinicos: The politics of *Marxism Today* ★

International Socialism 2:26 Spring 1985
Pete Green: Contradictions of the American boom ★ Colin Sparks: Labour and imperialism ★ Chris Bambery: Marx and Engels and the unions ★ Sue Cockerill: The municipal road to socialism ★ Norah Carlin: Is the family part of the superstructure? ★ Kieran Allen: James Connolly and the 1916 rebellion ★

International Socialism 2:25 Autumn 1984
John Newsinger: Jim Larkin, Syndicalism and the 1913 Dublin Lockout ★ Pete Binns: Revolution and state capitalism in the Third World ★ Colin Sparks: Towards a police state? ★ Dave Lyddon: Demystifying the downturn ★ John Molyneux: Do working class men benefit from women's oppression? ★

International Socialism 2:18 Winter 1983
Donny Gluckstein: Workers' councils in Western Europe ★ Jane Ure Smith: The early Communist press in Britain ★ John Newsinger: The Bolivian Revolution ★ Andy Durgan: Largo Caballero and Spanish socialism ★ M Barker and A Beezer: Scarman and the language of racism ★

International Socialism 2:14 Winter 1981
Chris Harman: The riots of 1981 ★ Dave Beecham: Class struggle under the Tories ★ Tony Cliff: Alexandra Kollontai ★ L James and A Paczuska: Socialism needs feminism ★ reply to Cliff on Zetkin ★ Feminists In the labour movement ★

International Socialism 2:13 Summer 1981
Chris Harman: The crisis last time ★ Tony Cliff: Clara Zetkin ★ Ian Birchall: Left Social Democracy In the French Popular Front ★ Pete Green: Alternative Economic Strategy ★ Tim Potter: The death of Eurocommunism ★

International Socialism 2:12 Spring 1981
Jonathan Neale: The Afghan tragedy ★ Lindsey German: Theories of patriarchy ★ Ray Challinor: McDouall and Physical Force Chartism ★ S Freeman & B Vandesteeg: Unproductive labour ★ Alex Callinicos: Wage labour and capitalism ★ Italian fascism ★ Marx's theory of history ★ Cabral ★

International Socialism 2:11 Winter 1980
Rip Bulkeley et al: CND In the 50s ★ Marx's theory of crisis and its critics ★ Andy Durgan: Revolutionary anarchism in Spain ★ Alex Callinicos: Politics or abstract thought ★ Fascism in Europe ★ Marilyn Monroe ★